WORKPLACE SAFETY: HOW TO MAKE IT NOT SUCK!

Your "Not-So-Secret" Guide to Engaging Employees and Driving Results

Lisa M. Buck, CSP®

Workplace Safety: How to Make It Not Suck! Your "Not-So-Secret" Guide to Engaging Employees and Driving Results

Copyediting by Rosalie Spear
Proofreading by Dr. Cheryl Mayfield, James and Gina Peters, and Jim Peters
Cover design by Joko Supomo

ISBN: 979-8-7374-5329-9
Version 1.0

DEDICATION

This book is dedicated to my husband, David Buck, for his undying love and support. My life is ridiculously better with him in it.

TABLE OF CONTENTS

ABOUT THE AUTHOR

Lisa Buck has over 20 years of experience in program development, leadership, safety manager mentorship, and most importantly, expertise in how to bring high energy and excitement to workplace safety. She is currently a corporate safety manager for a prominent beverage manufacturer leading 20 locations across multiple countries and continents. Lisa started her safety career in the pulp and paper industry before moving into food and beverage. As an environmental, health and safety manager she led thousands of workers to achieve world-class safety results.

Over the past decade, Lisa has also led two separate companies to Voluntary Protection Program (VPP) Star status in Nevada—a feat achieved solely by her in the State of Nevada. The VPP Star is the highest safety designation given by the Occupational Safety and Health Administration (OSHA). Other companies have since reached out to Lisa to provide pre-VPP audits and provide feedback so they, too, can achieve the coveted certification.

Lisa earned her BS from Columbia Southern University in Occupational Safety and Health. She holds the Certified Safety Professional® designation which is considered one of the highest safety designations in the industry. Lisa currently lives in Henderson, Nevada with her husband Dave and son, Connor.

FOREWORD

Safety is often not prioritized until it is too late, and an incident has occurred. But how can you get workers to be proactive instead of reactive? That is what this book is all about. Written by my amazing, smart sister, Lisa, this book will help you to energize and excite your staff in order to turn them into safety superheroes with a singular mission—to improve the culture of your workplace to ensure that everyone is safe!

Cheryl Mayfield

PREFACE

After spending many years as a safety professional and being lucky enough to work with some amazing people, I wanted to share my love for workplace safety with the world. I have learned many things the hard and slow way, but I want more for those that are just starting out or want to drive significant change in their role.

The purpose of this book is to motivate, excite, and educate readers to achieve an enviable safety culture with world-class safety results. After over 20 years in manufacturing as a safety professional, I have met and worked with both challenging and motivated people. In my career I have cried, laughed, rejoiced, and been extremely frustrated; but no matter the circumstance, my overarching goal is to always protect my employees/coworkers. When this can be done, I feel overjoyed, excited and proud.

Many times throughout my career, colleagues said, "You should write a book!" So, after years of jotting down ideas, talking with coworkers and colleagues, and mentoring new safety professionals, I did it!

Unlike other books on safety, I think you will find this book to be different and energizing. All of the ideas in this book have been proven by me (and sometime others) in real life within different facilities, companies, and industries. I am fortunate to have always had a great boss who allowed me to try new things and push the envelope.

I know I'm not your typical safety professional. I love games and rewards. I love to create special relationships with my team members—they must trust me to provide a safe workplace after all. I hope you find an idea or two in this book that you can implement at your workplace. You'll find ideas to engage your team, create the most amazing safety culture, and reap the rewards of lower incident rates.

During my quest to write this book, I was also finishing my bachelor's degree in occupational safety and health, raising a teenage son, traveling for work, running half marathons with my sister, and attempting to spend time with my family and friends. I am so lucky to have the support of my family, especially my husband, David Buck. I was able to spend time on my studies and write chapters in this book, while he did the dishes and laundry. He would bake me cookies and bring me the most incredible grilled cheese sandwiches while I studied for my next exam or read multiple chapters on industrial hygiene.

I also want to thank my father, Jim Peters, who is one of my best friends and biggest supporters. He has taught me to work hard, be my own unique person, and to not let anyone or anything stand in my way.

I am incredibly lucky to have the support of my brother and sister-in-law James and Gina Peters, who gave me advice and guidance during the creation of this book. James' book, *The Prosperity Track,* was the inspiration to get my ideas down on paper once and for all! I also want to thank my favorite sister Cheryl

Mayfield, who has allowed me to vent frustrations about work, school, certification exams, and this book. Both James and Cheryl have also been amazing editors, idea generators, and have allowed me to figure out what to say and how to say it.

I can't forget to recognize my children, Brianna Hile, Gabby Hile and her partner Chris, Connor Gagnon, Keegan Buck and his wife Rosalie, Cori Kertis and her husband Joe, and Kansas Buck and her partner Gage, who are a huge part of my life. I am excited to share my accomplishments with them as they are not only my kids, but my best friends. I am so lucky to have a blended family who supports me regardless of our bloodlines.

And lastly, I want to thank my friends, family, and coworkers for their unbelievable support while writing this book: DeAnne & Aldrick Lam, Mark Rauenzahn, Amanda Harriger, Nick Marquart, Carter Fahy, Rachel Rogers, Isabel Reyes, Kim Berry, Aileen Pla, Kari Schuster, Alanna Donovan, Jordan Schoyen, Dave Bain, Cindy Eccles, Kym Heckman, Ron Bongat, Pat Cholewa, Misty Reed, Diane Shapiro, Martin Olson, Gary Blosl, Rhonda Platzer, and Azure White.

And although she is in heaven, I want to shout out to my mama, Marlene Peters, who gave me my crazy personality, good looks ☺, an incredible love for my family, and the quest for a good bargain.

INTRODUCTION

Many workers, supervisors, and managers think workplace safety sucks. The many rules and regulations to follow make it the un-fun thing to do. In this book, readers will discover ways to create and implement an enviable safety culture where workers and leaders willingly engage in compliance, and have a little fun doing it.

There are hundreds, if not thousands, of books on this subject, but this one provides multiple examples of actual, implementable activities. Instead of just answers, it's chock full of real-life experiences that detail why workplace safety is important and how each reader can make a change in their workplace.

Readers will find pages of activities to get employees engaged in the safety program therefore driving improvement in the overall culture. Culture is way too hard to measure and some use tools like surveys and questionnaires to determine if workers are engaged. There is only one real way to measure if employees are engaged and that is through participation in the program. Various examples will be provided in this book to help safety leaders determine if employees are involved and if it is impacting their overall safety culture. I want readers to know why we must focus on behavior, rewards and recognition, and engaging employees. Compliance with the regulations is not enough. Knowing how to engage workers and get them to behave safely when you aren't looking is super important and isn't going to be found in an Occupational Safety and Health Administration (OSHA) book. Readers will discover what they can do to impact even a small number of employees to develop awesome partners in safety.

My website: LisaKnowsSafety.com is also an excellent source of information including forms and templates mentioned throughout this book. Be sure to check the website frequently for new information as I regularly provide updates.

I am so excited to share more than two decades of experiences, challenges, and successes with readers as we delve into the most exciting life of a safety professional!

SAFETY SUCKS – WHY NO ONE LIKES SAFETY

My first job in safety was in 1999 at a paper converting plant and my grandfather was not impressed with my interest in workplace safety. He worked in the steel mills for 40 years during the times when there were no safety rules and very few regulatory requirements. I was ecstatic to announce to my family that I had been promoted to Behavioral Safety Coordinator in charge of a behavioral observation program. Although my family was thrilled with my interest in safety, my grandfather, Ray, was dumbfounded. He proceeded to tell me how OSHA shut down his plant operations due to unsafe working conditions. I was confused. Why would he be upset about that? He proceeded to tell me that he made a very good living, pensions from both companies, and those hazards were "just part of the job."

I have to say I was stunned by his words. Grandpa Ray was telling me that he was willing to risk his life to make a living. But, this wasn't the military or police work, war or otherwise. He joked that his hearing loss prepared him for a long marriage to my grandmother. He wouldn't have to listen to Jeopardy or People's Court because he couldn't hear well after nearly 40 years of exposure to loud noise. As we all know, hearing loss can be more frustrating for the person talking than the person listening.

Grandpa Ray's comments didn't discourage me from attempting to improve the safety results in my new role. However, it did prepare me for the challenging group of people that I would soon encounter. I was a young, motivated person who fully believed in protecting people from workplace hazards. I learned very quickly to adjust my style to ask questions, learn from those in their jobs for decades, and that changing a safety culture takes time—lots of time.

Just wanting the culture to change wasn't enough. I tried training and face-to-face coaching, but it wasn't as successful as I had hoped. I found that people think safety sucks. Although most people want to be protected, they do not want to always do what is necessary to protect themselves. Employees want it easy, quick, and non-invasive. Great—just what safety is not. Confined space permits and testing is not easy or quick and wearing a respirator is invasive.

I pondered what I could do to make safety not suck. How could I make it exciting, fun, interactive, non-invasive, and still get the necessary results? It took me a long time to figure this out, decades actually. I learned the hard way in many instances—not everyone was as excited about safety as I was. But the years of experience and exposure gave me insight and taught me how to make workplace safety more attractive to workers, managers, and leaders.

Not everyone wants the same thing or is motivated by what motivates me or my boss. Workers may want to save time and receive accolades for a job well done. Managers want a reduction in workers' compensation costs and more profits for the company. Leaders are those that want to set the direction of safety in the company and then do what they say they are going to do—lead.

At times, workers, managers, and leaders may be frustrated by the results or lack thereof and I can relate to all of them! After many years of teaching, setting policies, writing reports, crunching numbers, and leading safety, I can tell you that there is one trait that a safety professional must have: **perseverance**. Don't stop just because the first attempt doesn't work. Don't give up when someone gets hurt. Use these as opportunities to reassess and adjust your direction and action plan. Remember that one data point does not make a trend. However, if near-misses, injuries, or property damage incidents continue to happen there is a problem in the system. You must stop and think about where the link is broken. There is a barrier somewhere preventing you from reaching the goal.

Think about your safety goal or action plan as a running track that has many hurdles. Runners don't jump over all the hurdles at one time; they take each one as an individual challenge. Each hurdle may represent a program, person, or behavioral challenge that you must face. Although you may want to go fast due to the nature of workplace safety and preventing injuries, you will just end up running through the hurdles and have to go back and stand them up again. In order to "clear" each hurdle, think about ways to eliminate the hurdle, so that it doesn't impede your path in the future.

So, why does workplace safety usually suck, and employees not want to do it? This may be different for your workplace, but I can tell you from the many safety professionals I have worked with and organizations I have audited it is pretty common—safety is hard. It is also complicated, full of rules, and not fun. Who wants to do something that is hard, complicated, full of rules, and not fun? Imagine hanging up a sign-up list for an activity and your advertisement to entice people to join is "Sign up HERE for an activity that is not-fun and hard." How many takers would you get? (Ok, maybe that grumpy guy from night shift. He seems to exude a feeling of not-fun.) With that being said, you can now see all the work to be done!

If we focus on creating a culture where workplace safety is easy (or at least easier), fun, and rewarding, then a lot more people will sign up.

Think about an employee on night shift who requires a face shield to perform a specific task. If that employee needs to go to the storeroom, look up the item number and location, find the face shield, check it out using an electronic system, and then finally go back to his work center—how likely is he to go and get the face shield? Does his supervisor recognize and commend him for a job well done?

In this example, we made it difficult for the employee to perform his job safely. We also gave him no positive recognition for working safely. These are the two main things we need to satisfy (ease of compliance and recognition) for employees to have an engaging and rewarding culture.

In order to improve an overall safety program, the hard stuff like culture, behaviors, and positive recognition must be addressed. Some of you might feel overwhelmed already! But don't fret—I have suggestions and plans that will help you achieve greatness! Each positive change will pay dividends and enhance your program, and each person you can get on your side will help drive this.

I have always been interested in workplace safety to protect my coworkers from industrial dangers. There are many people just like me (and you) who are interested in working safely and protecting others, too. It is important we connect with these like-minded people to tap into their knowledge, and most of all, their drive for greatness. Who doesn't want to be on the winning team?

In the coming chapters, I will help you develop an action plan, and identify potential hurdles and how to address them. You certainly may be able to "clear" a few small hurdles at a time, but remember to really focus on the larger, looming challenges. These challenges usually rear their ugly head in many different forms besides safety. I will also help you create some fun things to do that encourage employees to participate; these activities work by identifying and correcting hazards or at-risk behaviors.

Are you ready? Let's GO!

Step up to
the plate.
Become
a safety
advocate.

MOTIVATING THE UNMOTIVATED

I once interviewed a millwright who had 30+ years of experience working in the pulp and paper industry. His words stuck with me from the first moment we spoke. He was a burly man with rough hands and a deep voice. Retirement was nearing, and he had not always been an advocate of safety. During his many years of experience, he saw several of his coworkers injured and some involved in workplace fatalities. He paid close attention to the contributing factors that were communicated to the hourly workers after each incident, and he discovered a pattern. Each injured worker owned their personal safety. They had some level of culpability for their injury.

He remembered losing a friend in a workplace incident when his friend took a shortcut and bypassed a safety guard. That worker was pulled into a piece of equipment and crushed to death. Although he didn't witness the incident, he immediately knew what happened. He himself had removed that same guard to access the equipment rather than shut it down. At times he felt invincible and thought those types of incidents don't happen to trained workers like him. But they do and it did.

After hearing of the fatality and learning it was his friend, who happened to be only a few months from retirement, he began to look at things differently. Was it worth it? Rushing or removing a guard to save a few minutes? His friend is missing his retirement now—something he worked his whole life for, and instead lost his life in an instant.

I asked him what he did differently after that day. What he told me was surprising. **He immediately joined the safety committee and took on guarding improvements.** How could physical machine guards be modified or improved to allow for lubrication, troubleshooting, or inspection? He learned how to engineer out hazards and thought of additional ways to conduct tasks, like vibration analysis and lubrication from outside the equipment or remotely. Yes, some of it cost money, but not nearly as much as the cost of a worker dying. He was going to spend his last few months on the job protecting himself and others so they, too, would get to enjoy their retirement.

Stepping up to the plate and acting as a safety advocate wasn't easy for this millwright. His coworkers thought he was a traitor. His bosses thought he had lost his mind, but he intended to make it to retirement and take the rest of the guys with him. What moved me most about this worker was his courage and strength. He said he cried some nights; not because he had a hard day or that his body hurt (although it did), but because he was scared. He was scared that it was too late to correct all the hazards that even he himself had ignored for years. He was in maintenance after all—the department everyone counted on to repair and eliminate hazards. He was embarrassed by his behavior and wanted to make amends.

We talked for a long time about making a plan and sticking to it. The plan is never hard; we always have grand ideas of what we want to do. It's the follow-through that's difficult. Getting the work done with limited funds and resources, unmotivated workers, and most of all a lack of leadership was going to be hard. After listening to the agony and embarrassment in his voice, I had more determination and strength than ever to follow through with my own plan: a plan to change the culture and the way workers think. How on Earth would I do it?

In a department of just one person, it was going to be hard; but after talking with my new friend the millwright, I realized I had the answer. I could build my safety army just like he did. **He was able to change the mindset of his coworkers by finding what motivated them—retirement.**

They say motivation comes from within, but I don't believe that's 100 percent true. I believe that workers are motivated by many different competing priorities.

For example, if someone is money motivated and receives a paycheck for going to work, will they show up every day knowing they will get paid? Not necessarily. They may also think about staying home to spend time with their family, because they have competing priorities. However, if a family member falls ill and extra money is needed to pay for medical bills, they may work overtime.

When it comes to workplace safety, workers mentally weigh competing priorities, even if they do it subconsciously. If a machine breaks down and it takes 10 minutes to walk back to the shop to get their lockout locks, will they go get them? Or will they jump right in to service the machine to save time? They want to fix the machine, and they want to do it quickly. How do we go about addressing those things?

First, we can address and eliminate any barriers. If employees had immediate access to their lockout locks, they would not have to retrieve them, saving time. When supervisors and managers are supportive, provide assistance, and give positive recognition for safe behaviors it builds worker confidence.

"I saw you go get your lockout locks, Dave, and lockout the machine before performing maintenance. I appreciate you taking the time to do your work safely." These words can make all the difference when workers are under pressure to get the job done. If they only hear a manager tapping their foot behind them, they are more likely to make a critical and unfortunate error or shortcut.

Are you a manager, supervisor, or leader in your organization? How often do you praise your workers for taking the time to perform their work safely? Do you feel it is just something they are supposed to do? A job expectation? Consider changing your mindset.

Workplace safety should not just be considered a job expectation or condition of employment. Think of it like this: workplace safety is a value we are not willing to compromise.

You may not agree. You may think that the rules are the rules and workers should follow those rules, but that really isn't the case. If you have children or have been around children, you don't just tell them the rules. They will almost always ask, "Why?"

Why do I have to wear a coat? Why do I have to go to school? The same goes for adults! *Why must I lockout this machine before I perform maintenance? Why must I fill out a permit to perform hot work?*

If you get over the fact that workers aren't inherently a pain in the butt, you'll soon understand what motivates workers. They need to know **why**!

Workers also need to know what *you* value. You can't just say it—talk is cheap. You must act. **You must physically acknowledge what you value.** Shake someone's hand, give them a thumbs up, and tell them you appreciate them wearing their respirator properly. Put something in writing: a note, an email, or card telling the worker how quickly they were able to get the machine back up and running while locking it out. A small token, a certificate, or other physical items are great mementos that someone can show their family.

Do your workers only show their family their exhaustion, bruises, and injuries they receive at work? Is that all they have to remember the workplace? Is that all their children will remember?

Safety is not the responsibility of just the safety professional; it is **everyone's** responsibility. Think about new employees for a moment, especially the younger generation. They are so impressionable, and it is critical that they learn the correct and safe way of doing things from their experienced coworkers. It is difficult, but we must ensure our experienced workers are setting the safe example right from the start.

I remember a time during a paper machine outage when an experienced millwright was giving advice to another, less experienced maintenance worker. He was telling him where to stand while they were rigging a very heavy roll to be lifted with a crane. The inexperienced worker said, "I know," and kept working, but was too close to the roll that was going to be lifted. The millwright stopped the work, pulled the worker aside, and explained that he may feel comfortable being that close, but that is not how they did things. They worked as a team, and everyone had to agree that it was safe to lift the roll before they began the lift.

He walked him back over to the area where they were working and showed him what could happen should the straps break during the lift. The inexperienced worker understood and thanked him for taking the time to show him the right place to stand.

Now, getting a paper machine up and running can be a chaotic time, but this millwright knew the importance of taking just a few minutes to teach the correct and safe way to perform the lift. And of course, I commended the millwright for being an amazing leader!

Summary

- Giving effective praise doesn't come naturally for everyone, including supervisors, managers, and leaders. **An important aspect of praise is to do it when you see the work.** Don't wait a day, a week, or longer. Stop what you are doing and acknowledge the work that someone has done.
- A high-five, handshake, or even a smile goes a long way. If a more significant acknowledgement is warranted, then follow up with a token of appreciation.

In the following chapters, I share additional personal stories and examples that help guide you. You will read not only about positive experiences, but some of the challenges I faced and overcame.

Creating an enviable safety culture starts with laying the foundation.

WHAT IS SAFETY CULTURE?

Businesses "prioritize" safety results yet often don't know how, or don't try hard enough, to actually obtain them. It takes years to create and maintain a solid, high-performing safety culture. All employees from the highest-ranking manager to the newest hire must understand the company's view of safety.

Your company's safety culture is important to your customers, employees, and the entire business as a whole. An amazing safety culture can positively impact your business by driving engagement, reducing workers' compensation claims/costs, and attracting the very best talent. Safety leaders in the organization must define **what the culture is now,** *and* **how they wish to transform it.** Read on to discover ways to assess the current culture, and identify those surmountable barriers that will no longer stop you from having a sought-after, safe workplace.

Creating an enviable safety culture starts with laying the foundation. It is critical to set up some basic management systems in order to handle the influx of opportunity. For instance, if you want employees to report hazards or risks, you must have a system to document the initial report and track follow-up actions.

Be prepared to handle the workload on the journey to a better safety culture!

For example, a company I worked for already had a safety work order system in place, so I began drumming up business for the safety program by encouraging employees to report risks using this system. In the first year, we had **hundreds** of safety work orders and it was super challenging to address them all!

With the help of the maintenance team, we developed a strategy to categorize the work orders, get the employees involved in the corrective action, and put together plans for capital requests.

When employees saw their request was fulfilled, they felt encouraged to look for more potential risks. This process eventually led to identifying ways to reduce risk and prevent injuries, not simply fix or repair broken equipment.

As safety professionals, we can sometimes come across as the people who create barriers to faster production. **Creating a partnership between safety department personnel and all other departments is extremely critical** to creating a successful safety culture. It is a tough balance; employee's concerns must be heard, yet the entire responsibility of addressing those concerns cannot be placed solely on the shoulders of the safety department. This takes a commitment from department managers and the head honcho—whoever that might be!

Since many safety programs don't have a full-time safety manager or even a safety department, it becomes the responsibility of the person who knows the most about safety.

At one point in his career, my husband, Dave, started a job with a new company as a maintenance and facilities manager.

The company didn't have a local safety person, but there was a designated, corporate safety person and they resided in another state, in another time zone.

Dave was cast into the role of safety leader because he knew so much about workplace safety from his previous roles (and from being married to an amazing safety lady!).

Now, his normal role as maintenance and facilities manager would have him leading safety for his department and being a good role model for the rest of the facility; however, in this case he was spending time organizing safety data sheets, ordering PPE, and scheduling CPR and first aid training. The problem is, that he was unable to really focus on developing programs, encouraging participation, and auditing the facility for compliance. He was doing what he could to establish a foundation, but without a full-time person, it was difficult at best.

In some cases, especially for small companies, it may not be necessary to have a dedicated, full-time safety person; but, in the absence of a safety professional, there must be clear expectations of who is handling each program. There must also be specific roles and responsibilities to ensure compliance with the ridiculous amount of paperwork, inspections, and audits that each program requires.

So, what does a facility or company need to do to create an enviable safety culture? What does an enviable safety culture look like? As we continue this chapter, I'll tell you how to identify attributes of this illustrious and sought-after culture and how to capture it yourself.

My first bit of advice is to start with an evaluation of the overall safety program. By determining where the safety program is and what needs to be fixed, you'll be able to start with the foundation and work your way up from there. Understanding employees' thoughts on workplace safety will help you understand the current safety culture. As with any issue, you first must discover what needs to be corrected, improved, or enhanced.

Surveys are one way to gain knowledge about how people feel, but these can be overwhelming or just plain boring. Good luck getting participation, workers can be easily annoyed with surveys, because they rarely see anything done with the data gathered from them. This is, unfortunately, all so true!

Another way, and frankly the best way, would be to talk to employees and ask them questions such as:

- What do you think our biggest challenges are in the safety program?
- What could we do to make it easier to comply?
- What would you be willing to do differently to improve results?
- Have you ever participated in the safety committee? If so, why do you participate? If not, why haven't you?
- Do you think you have all the information needed to do your job safely? What information does someone in your position need in order to be safe doing this job?

Notice that in the first two questions I used "our" and "we" to demonstrate the shared ownership of the safety program.

At one of my safety positions in manufacturing, I decided to talk to each and every employee over the course of a month. I felt that giving each employee face time would be much more accurate and informative than a survey, and would allow for follow-up questions. Fortunately, the facility was small enough to manage this task. Most employees were willing to give me feedback on the overall program, and suggestions regarding things that needed to be fixed or changed.

A few employees were not willing to say anything negative about the program or company, as they felt there would be retaliation. This was disheartening, but I made note of those employees and felt that I could circle back with them after a few months to see if their view had changed. Some employees even walked in the other direction when I approached or pretended not to see me. They didn't even know my intentions, and you could tell they didn't want to find out!

One interesting tidbit I learned was concerning the safety committee. Some employees stated that they didn't participate, because no one asked them! The committee would also implement changes without asking for feedback or suggestions, so workers were understandably frustrated.

Other employees stated that they made suggestions for improvement, but their feedback fell on deaf ears. **Employees were even willing to do the work and make the improvements, but no one followed through.**

One employee, Frank, made it a point to show me a few suggestions he had made that would not only improve the safety of a particular task, but it would shorten the time it took to perform a changeover of the equipment to a different package configuration. If we would move an adjustment knob from inside the equipment, to the outside of the equipment, the employee would not have to lockout the energy sources, thus saving time and making it safer.

The cost was very low, and the return was very high; the payback would be realized in only the first few changeovers. I could see that if we could get to a point where employee's suggestions were reviewed, considered, and implemented (when possible), we could begin to foster a partnership that encourages suggestions and improves production and employee safety.

Many employees also stated that, at times, management also made it difficult to comply. When I asked what would make it easier to comply, a few of the answers were an easy fix.

One employee, Amanda, told me to stock the correct sizes of PPE. As a smaller person, size XL-4X chemical suits are too big and bulky, and it actually creates more of a hazard wearing it.

Another employee, Kim, told me that many of the tools are too far away from where workers needed them. If we relocated the necessary tools to the correct location, it would make it easier to make the right choice every time.

Don't get me wrong, I got a lot of comments like, "Pay me more money" or "Give me more days off." To these, I simply explained that I could only work on the things I had control over.

From interviewing staff, I learned that the baseline for the safety culture was low. I also learned some of the reasons why the current situation made for a weak safety culture. The best thing I found out was that the employees were not only identifying the problems, but had suggestions on how to fix them!

So, what makes a great safety culture? It depends on who you ask.

I took the opportunity to ask my fellow safety peeps what they thought, and their answers are below:

- "Powerful safety cultures are built on three elements—commitment, ownership, and trust. Commitment makes it mine and develops personal expectations. Ownership makes it ours and prioritizes people over process. Trust moves us in the same direction together. The best safety cultures understand each element, how they are integral to the others, and how to constantly nourish them to grow the strongest possible team."—Nick Marquart, Environmental, Health and Safety Manager
- "A great safety culture is manifested by people truly feeling cared for by their organization and replicating that ethic. It's about people being listened to, and in turn being willing to listen to others when identifying and addressing hazards at work. It's a mindset that puts people ahead of profits and one that communicates consistent expectations about safe behaviors from the CEO as well as the line worker. Lastly, it's one where people are held accountable for their actions, but not without first being given the tools and training to set themselves up for success."—Carter Fahy, Senior Manager of Environmental, Health, Safety and Security
- "In order to achieve a great safety culture, management and leadership must play an active role in demonstrating that the safety of their employees is the company's top priority. Employees should never be made to feel that production takes priority over working safely. Employees should be involved in the process to get their buy-in. They need to feel that their opinions,

concerns, and ideas are being listened to, matter, and can make a difference."—Alanna Donovan, Environmental, Health and Safety Manager

- "A dynamic safety culture needs to be grown through leadership, commitment, and engagement. A safety leader takes safety beyond compliance and recognizes the importance of each individual on the job. Ultimately, beyond all the policies and procedures are the people. Commitment requires one to not only talk the talk but walk the walk. It is one thing to **say** that safety is a priority; it is another thing to **show** that it is. When it comes to safety, actions truly speak louder than words. An engaged workforce encourages workers to make suggestions, participate in safety activities, mentor new employees, and take ownership of their own safety. The goal is to continue to improve, to make sure everyone feels responsible for safety."—Jordan Schoyen, Environmental, Health and Safety Specialist

Although safety professionals, leaders, and managers have differing opinions about what a great safety culture looks like, we all want to be able to **observe behaviors and measure actions.**

Let's start with observing behaviors. When I think about the behaviors I want to observe, I think about not only body language, but spoken words. As I have mentioned previously, employees nearly ran away when I approached the production area; that is not a behavior I want to observe! We should be seeking a partnership in safety where employees embrace our presence and that of management. Employees must understand that the outcome of our visit is to seek suggestions, or to praise them for a job well done. Or, if it is to review poor performance, it is done in a way to encourage the employee to improve their behavior with the assistance of their manager.

When we seek suggestions or feedback from employees, we want to ensure they are not frustrated with the safety program. How do we do that?

Think about a time when you approached an employee that was frustrated. You can physically observe their frustration. Their eyebrows furrow, eyes roll, or they sigh deeply. (This might actually be the daily reaction of my teenage son!) We are seeking the exact opposite of that reaction.

When we speak to employees about safety, we want to observe them smiling, nodding their heads, and/or providing suggestions for improvement. Keeping employees smiling and engaged in safety doesn't come easy, and can be troublesome if you don't honor your commitments. Providing updates on safety improvements, giving employees an opportunity to participate in decision-making, and sharing successes will help you stay connected to your employees.

Many hourly workers just want to be heard and for management to consider their feedback. When I first started asking employees for feedback and suggestions, I again spoke to Frank. He told me that he made a suggestion to improve the safety in an area during a safety meeting, after there had been a few incidents. The previous safety manager did nothing with his suggestions. Frank simply wanted to know if his feedback was considered. He would understand if his idea wasn't feasible, but he never received feedback either way. After a few other suggestions were treated in the same manner, he stopped providing feedback and participating.

His feedback to me was to provide updates either way. If changes cannot not be implemented due to cost or difficulty, then just be honest and tell the team. On the other hand, if changes will be implemented, then tell employees what will be done.

Frank said it motivated him when he made a suggestion and saw it come to fruition in his work area. He felt as though his opinion mattered, and that he was part of a team that valued safety and input from the employees.

Another observable way to determine if your safety culture is enviable is to **listen to employees describe or talk about the safety program.** When visitors, vendors, or contractors come to your site, listen to your employees talk about safety.

I recently had to meet with the management team of a contractor, after they had not met their obligations to perform work safely while on our property. The maintenance manager, Kari, and I met with the owner and supervisor of the company and explained why we were having the meeting. I asked the supervisor if Jesse, our project engineer, could have done a better job explaining our expectations.

He said, "No. Jesse was very clear on the safety expectations of your company. He made himself available all day and asked our team members if there was anything he could do to help. We take full responsibility for the actions of our employees while performing work on your property."

This was a profound statement. It confirmed that although the safety manager cannot be everywhere at once, the team is still doing what we ask of them making it abundantly clear what our expectations are as a company. As safety leaders, we expect our team to be part of the solution; we must do more than explain the expectations and walk away. We want our team to be partners in safety with everyone who we interact with, on a daily basis.

Although I didn't observe Jesse explaining our expectations or talking with workers throughout the day, I received the feedback which confirmed our commitment.

On a separate occasion, I had the opportunity to observe another employee discussing the safety committee with a new employee. The new employee, Scott, was asking a seasoned employee, Aileen, if there was a safety committee to join. Aileen explained that yes, there was a safety committee, and they met monthly. She also explained that there were high expectations of the safety committee members and this wasn't like any other safety committee she had been part of.

Other safety committee members nearby started to laugh and verbally agreed with what Aileen was saying. She went on to explain that the committee was a highly regarded team that gathered suggestions for improvement from their departments, completed monthly homework, and was expected to report their assignment's progress. Scott had a concerned look on his face after hearing the details about the committee responsibilities. Aileen then explained there were many benefits to being part of the committee and talked about the fun and rewards, too. She told him that being part of a winning team takes a lot of work, but it was worth it.

Scott said he was totally into winning teams and would join her at the next meeting! This is another example of employees talking to other employees about the successes of the safety committee or safety program. It is critical that employees speak positively about safety whether you are around or not.

Now that we've discussed observing behaviors, we need to talk about measuring actions. There are so many ways that we can measure what we do regarding safety, but I'll include a few examples to explain the purpose.

First, let's focus on hourly employees and what they might want us to measure. As I mentioned earlier, Frank was frustrated at the lack of communication regarding suggestions for improvement, and the lack of actual improvement taking place.

In many of the manufacturing sites I have worked, we measured safety-related work orders. These work orders were corrective action items that were entered into a software/database, and "coded" to inform the maintenance team of the potential to expedite the work. The work order system provided a way for team members to enter a work request to address a hazard or risk. The maintenance manager or maintenance planner would then receive a notification from the system that a safety-related work order had been requested. However, hourly employees had previously entered safety-related work orders that sat in the system for months, **even years**, without being completed!

If you have a similar system, **ensure there are standards to address safety-related work orders within a specified time.** If, for example, your team decides that all safety work requests deemed necessary must be completed within 1-3 days, then a policy or procedure should document the expectations.

You may also have different levels of safety requests. Your procedures should outline the difference between an immediate risk, and a general safety improvement that will reduce the likelihood of an incident. These procedures should be documented so everyone in the organization is operating from the same sheet of music.

An additional way to measure actions is from participation. Activities that employees participate in, such as safety committee meetings, monthly challenges, or training opportunities, should be measured and communicated. Report on metrics such as percentage of participation by the facility or department, safety committee meeting attendance by month or by year, and monthly participation. You will be able to see a trend whether your program participation is staying the same, growing, or declining.

It also shows other leaders where they can focus their efforts, especially if their department is lacking compared to others. This is a good way to instill a little bit of healthy competition amongst the teams as well.

Communicating other measurable actions like injury and illness data, before-and-after pictures from an improvement event, or progress toward company or department goals will help employees stay informed.

If you have a safety bulletin board, you know it is not only difficult to keep it updated, but challenging to get employees to read the information. You will never be able to make employees read the information, but you can create a challenge that has employees reviewing the information.

When you think about it, **what's in it for the employee**? What is the incentive to know the information on your bulletin board?

If there is critical information that I want employees to know, **I create a fill-in-the-blank challenge**. Employees grab a paper form from a designated location and use the information on the bulletin board to fill in the blanks. I collect all the forms by a specified deadline and then raffle off some cool company swag for a few winners. Everyone who participates gets a candy bar or token (see "Show Me the Money" chapter on this topic), which provides a small incentive to participate again. Who doesn't love a free Twix® or Reece's® Peanut Butter Cup?

Employees learn the information and have a little fun doing it. Plus. they are then also able to spread the information to their coworkers.

Summary

Let's review what a safety culture is and how to measure it for success.

- First, establish some basic management systems. These systems must be in place so that once you begin to drum up business for reporting and correcting hazards, and tracking participation, you have a system to help you work efficiently.
- Second, talk to employees to find out what they think about the safety program. You must know what needs to be fixed from their perspective, too.
- Third, provide feedback on suggestions for improvement, even if you decide not to implement the change. Workers want to know what is going on with their ideas.
- Fourth, do what you say you are going to do—follow through—on your commitments. This one is hard, but oh so worth it!

- Fifth, listen to what your workers are saying about the safety program. Do they speak highly about the work that is being done or improvements that are made? Or are they frustrated? Use this as feedback to change direction if necessary.
- Lastly, measure the actions you put in place. Don't just throw a bunch of stuff at the wall. Ensure you are working on solutions that will address the above-mentioned issues.

In the following chapters, we'll dive into more depth on successful safety committees, participation, and creating an action plan to implement at your site. These, too, will help you develop an enviable safety culture!

Ask safety
committee
members
to sign a
commitment
letter.

DO WE REALLY NEED A SAFETY COMMITTEE?

I know what you're probably thinking - what should a safety committee do? What should a successful safety committee look like? When you think of a successful safety committee, what is it NOT?

It isn't a meeting to complain. It isn't opinions and negative talk. It also shouldn't be a meeting that workers have to attend but rather want to attend! And it certainly isn't a place where employees come to find fault in the company or bash management.

In order to ensure you get a dedicated group of workers that want to accomplish the safety goals and objectives, you need to tell them a few things. **I ask each of my safety committee members to sign a commitment letter** (see example in this chapter and on LisaKnowsSafety.com).

Although the commitment letter is never used for disciplinary action, it is a list of expectations that each committee member will be asked to meet and uphold. I allow all employees to drop in and attend a safety committee meeting, but to be considered a committee member, I must have their commitment in writing. If you want to create a committee that employees view as a respected, cohesive team that gets things done, then you need something tangible.

A few things to consider including in your commitment letter are: attending meetings, conducting quarterly inspections, participating in monthly safety activities, and performing monthly behavioral safety observations. After employees review and sign the commitment letter, they receive a badge (see picture) that can be purchased online or made by using a laminator.

The badge is a tangible item that states they are a safety committee member. During new hire orientation, I tell workers to look for the badge if they ever have a concern or question about safety. It has helped to provide a "safety partner" for new employees who may never have worked in a similar environment, or been exposed to specific hazards.

At times, new employees may need to locate PPE or have a question about when a specific inspection is required. It's important to have multiple safety partners throughout the facility that are engaged and happy to help.

https://www.mysafetysign.com/badges/safety-committee-member-id-badge/sku-bd-0002?engine=google-base&keyword=ID+Badge+Bulldog+Clip&skuid=BD-0002-BD-3x2.125-Q5&gclid=Cj0KCQiAv6yCBhCLARIsABq-JTjZMQIugEFm_eVH-Q5PghMNyZIxJQFxVouidOmJ2P-KQe7PfO_iYFz1YaAkMiEALw_wcB

Safety Committee Member Commitment Letter

I, ______________________________, promise to commit and dedicate myself to the following responsibilities and expectations as a Safety Committee member:

- Be a role model and have a positive attitude toward safety.
- Attend monthly committee meetings.
- Assist in extra curricular activities planned and assigned by the committee and follow through to completion (audits, homework, inspections, etc.).
- Solicit crews for new ideas, safety issues, and concerns. Be visible and involve them in correcting safety concerns and/or audit items.
- Update crew at hand-off meetings – next shift after safety committee meeting and at other meetings as needed. Assist in leading shift or department safety meetings/discussions.
- Complete behavioral safety observation (BSO) each month.
- Assist others in meeting their personal goals in regard to safety.
- Actively participate in all aspects. Pursue and/or suggest improvements.

By signing this form, I acknowledge that I am committing to the above responsibilities and expectations for a period of one (1) year starting ____________________.

______________________________ Committee Member Signature

______________________________ EH&S Manager Signature

_______________ Date

I also ask seasoned committee members to mentor newer members by checking in with them occasionally to provide guidance or reinforce our committee goals. I have observed many of our new members meeting with our seasoned members to discuss expectations, getting their team involved, and how to address specific concerns. It is an awesome feeling to see the team come together to help the entire facility.

Monthly Meetings

One way I get my safety committee involved is to start each meeting with "Why do I Participate?" This activity confirms, each month, the reasons why we participate in the safety committee. I typically lead an activity or discussion about what is important to each of us. The employees love these and look forward to each meeting to see what activities are planned.

A few examples of activities are:

- Give each safety committee member a straw, an empty paper cup, and another cup filled with chocolate candies such as M&Ms®. Tell the members they have been injured in a workplace incident, and both hands were injured. Their doctor has issued them restrictions that include "no use of both hands." Now, give them 60 seconds to transfer the candies from the full cup to the empty cup using only the straw - no use of either hand. After the activity, explain that rather than pouring the candies from one cup to the other, the task is much more difficult when you can't use your hands.

- Break up the safety committee into two groups. Give each member five Hershey Kisses®. Give the first person on each team a set of oven mitts. Once the activity begins, the first team member will attempt to open all five of his candies with the oven mitts on his/her hands. Once they are all open, they pass the oven mitts to the next person. This continues until one team has all their Kisses® open. This activity is another example of not being able to use the hands to complete a task. It also represents the use of incorrectly sized PPE!
- Prepare for this activity by obtaining several locks and keys (such as those used for lockout/tagout). Also, prep a pair of goggles or a face shield by scratching them, or using a black marker to obscure vision when using the PPE. Put all the miscellaneous keys into a box so that members will have to sort through it, searching for the correct key for their lock. Again, split the group into two teams and give each safety committee member a lock. The first person in the group will put on the damaged PPE and sort through the box, trying to match up the correct key for their lock. Once they get their lock unlocked, they pass the damaged PPE and box of remaining keys to the next person. This is a great example of how frustrating damaged or dirty PPE can be, and the effect of not keeping tools and supplies organized.
- Purchase several sets of chopsticks, and give one pair to each safety committee member. Also, give each member 20 Tic Tac® candies and a plastic cup. Each team member will turn the cup upside down and have 30 seconds to pick up the candies from the table with their chopsticks, and place them on the upside-down cup. This activity focuses on using the right tool for the job.

- Give each member a die (which I purchased in bulk online), an empty cup, and a cup of mini marshmallows. Write the game rules on the board, and make them somewhat confusing. The rules could be something like: "Even numbers move one marshmallow to the empty cup except for the number two, then move one back into the full cup. Odd numbers move two marshmallows into the empty cup, except for the number five, then move three marshmallows back into the full cup." The purpose of this activity is to show the importance of communication and how even the simplest of messages can be misunderstood by workers.
- Give each member a blank piece of paper and a pen, and have them draw a safety warning label without using any words. After everyone is done, each member will pass their drawing to the left and describe the warning. I did this activity to explain that many new pieces of equipment are delivered to a facility with warnings that workers do not understand or are confusing.

All of these examples are completed with participants sitting down to prevent injuries to committee members! If at any time someone does not feel they can perform one of the tasks, I do not make them.

Many of the supplies I purchased were used several times (chopsticks, dice, locks, etc.) and made it easy to determine what activities to conduct in the coming months. The overall purpose is to engage employees in the program and connect them to the work. The day after every safety committee meeting, I go into the lunchroom and listen to hourly safety committee members sharing their stories with the other team members. They always had a message—they weren't simply stating we played a game in the meeting.

Again, the purpose is to not just lecture about safety results and challenges; it's to connect the workers to why we care about safety and making improvements. Workers are much more likely to remember an event, task, or game than they are a lecture. The connection is so important, and many additional games or ideas can be found with a simple internet search.

Accountability is another tough challenge when it comes to a successful safety committee. Creating an **attendance tracker** (see example in this chapter and on LisaKnowsSafety.com) and tying rewards to attendance at safety committee meetings is an excellent way to give members another reason to attend and participate.

Give members a little nudge to get out of bed on their day off to attend a safety committee meeting by offering a chance at earning a reward. For example, I explained that safety committee members would receive a jacket when they attended ten safety committee meetings. The meetings did not have to be consecutive and they could take longer than a year. I created a spreadsheet to update each meeting, and safety committee members were always asking how close they were to earning their jacket.

The jackets were embroidered with the company logo and the words: "Safety Committee Member." When other employees saw the jackets, they too became enamored! The jackets were about $40 each and a fairly inexpensive way to get members to the meetings. Of course, only those full-fledged members who signed a commitment letter were eligible for the jacket.

As another incentive and way to participate, I introduced safety committee member homework. I had some highly motivated safety committee members that were interested to learn more and become better safety leaders. I talked with the plant leadership team about giving out some additional assignments, along with a small reward tied to homework completion. It was a such a big hit that I began giving out homework at each meeting. The homework was easy and voluntary to complete.

Safety Committee Member Attendance

Committee Members	Jan	Feb	Mar	Apr	May	Jun	Jul	Aug	Sep	Oct	Nov	Dec	**Total Meetings Attended**
													0
													0
													0
													0
													0
													0
													0
													0
													0
													0
													0
													0
													0
Total	0	0	0	0	0	0	0	0	0	0	0	0	0

It typically focused on a topic such as lockout/tagout, confined spaces, electrical safety, or machine guarding, and would be an activity to discuss risk or find solutions to current problems. Safety committee members who completed the homework would receive two tokens that could be used in the company reward store (more on this later).

Here are a few homework examples:

- Hand injuries have been a challenge for the site recently. What do you think are our biggest challenges? What could we change to make it easier for employees to complete specific tasks? Are the right gloves available for tasks utilizing chemicals?
- OSHA issued an updated National Emphasis Program focused on amputations in manufacturing. In your work area, are there any unguarded pinch points or other areas that may pose a hazard to employees?
- If you could identify one of your coworkers as a safety leader, who would it be and why? What do they do to make you think that way? Now, think of someone who is not a safety leader. What do they do to make them less than a safety leader? What behaviors do you observe that makes you think that way?
- If you were going to interview someone for a position in the safety department, what two critical questions would you ask them? What attributes should a safety leader have that would enable them to work cohesively with both the hourly workforce and management team?
- It's Hearing Health Month, and employees should be able to identify the proper hearing protection and how to wear it. Fill out the form by circling which picture illustrates hearing protection that is not appropriate (see example).

Turn in to ________ by ________________

Name: ____

Circle the items that do NOT represent good hearing protection!

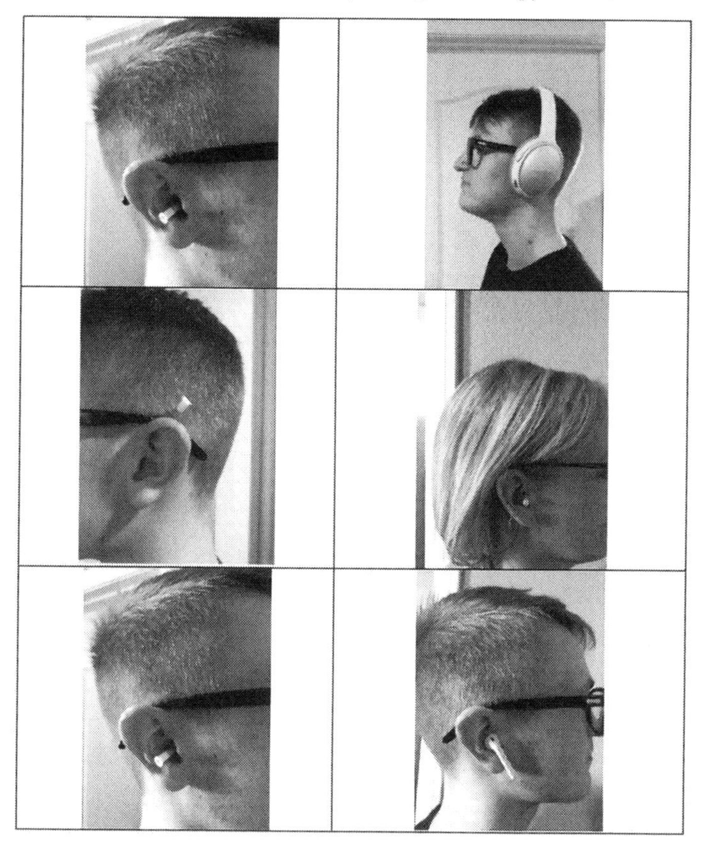

Continuing to motivate safety committee members year after year can be daunting. In order to keep them motivated and interested, they have to be challenged and rewarded. I find that breaking up the calendar year into sections can give you a starting point.

During the first quarter of each calendar year, I kick off safety committee meetings with a recap of the previous year. At one meeting I focus on successes by sharing before-and-after pictures of finished work, or projects that were completed safely (see pictures below).

At another meeting, I present injury and illness data from the previous year. Pairing this information with incident-contributing factors allows the committee to set an updated focus. The safety committee members should then participate in developing an action plan to address these contributing factors. If the primary contributing factors were failure to wear PPE, pedestrian and forklift driver at-risk interactions, and improper lockout/tagout procedures, the committee members can then brainstorm how to address each at-risk behavior. I will discuss action planning in more detail in the chapter, "Action Plans—Are They Really Needed?"

The second quarter of the year should be spent tackling action items and keeping track of progress. Many times, committees do an amazing job of developing a list of actions to complete, but don't follow through! It isn't any different than New Year's resolutions. We have grandiose ideas of losing weight, reorganizing closets, and starting projects, but many of these things never come to fruition. Keeping the list of actions updated and discussed at each meeting will prioritize its completion. Peter Drucker said, "What gets measured gets managed." This couldn't be more true!

The third quarter of the year should not only be focused on actions, but on current successes and challenges. What has the safety committee accomplished so far? Is the committee on track with actions, attendance, homework, etc.? How is the facility performing in relation to the safety goals? What are some obstacles the facility, safety committee, or departments have overcome? What milestones have been reached? A couple of example milestones could be the number of days without a lost time injury, or a record number of actions completed in a month?

It is so important to identify challenges, but to also celebrate the work that has been done and the journey along the way. Let's use the New Year's resolution to lose weight as an example. When someone wants to lose weight, they don't celebrate only when they have lost it **all**. They have celebrations throughout their weight-loss journey. Some may even have minor, or major, setbacks.

There are only two choices—give up or get going! If we give up, the only result is failure. If the committee works alongside the smaller teams in the facility to take action and address setbacks, the only result is success.

At one point, I had my safety committee working on a project to improve safety orientation for contractors. The project was expected to take a few months as we gathered ideas, observed contractors working, and reviewed audits previously completed by project managers. After the first month, I could tell that committee members were anxious during the regularly scheduled safety committee meeting. Frustrations were voiced, and facial expressions were strained. I had never seen the committee so disengaged.

One of the frustrations was that we had so much work to do to protect our own employees; why would we take the focus off them and instead put it on workers from another company? I immediately stopped the discussion and changed gears.

Utilizing the computer and projector, I pulled up OSHA's website and researched fatality reports. If you aren't familiar with OSHA's website, there is a section where they detail workplace fatalities and corresponding violations and citations issued. Some of the fatalities are contracted workers.

I found a few cases related to the type of work we did, and presented that information to the committee. One of the fatal injuries was an electrical contractor that fell through an unguarded opening onto a lower level. He was running electrical wire for a new installation before falling to his death.

Another fatality documented a host employer's worker who was struck by a forklift; the forklift was operated by a contracted worker. I explained how these types of fatal injuries can happen and still involve our employees.

If we develop a partnership with each worker on our site, we can create a collaborative safety culture where all lives are valued equally. After learning this, interest was sparked, and the committee started to ask questions.

As a team, we then discussed ways to keep it interesting, and how to not take on too much. We decided to break up the responsibilities, and assign tasks to smaller teams dedicated to specific issues. For example, one team would collect observation data and report back to the rest of the committee. Another team would reach out to our main contractors, and set up meetings to go over our updated expectations and orientation. As a team we needed to refocus and to get every member on board. By changing what we were working on and creating smaller teams, I was able to re-engage the committee members and set more easily obtainable goals.

My point to this story is to adjust your focus if things get stagnant, challenging, or overwhelming. Similar to a relationship, workout routine, or diet, we must make changes to keep it interesting. Safety committees are no different.

Lastly, rounding out the year is important to ensure a solid finish. Safety committee members must continue to report successes and communicate tasks that still need to be accomplished.

As an example, required training tends to be pushed to the last few months of the year due to scheduling conflicts or time constraints. This can cause chaos for safety professionals and the committee! To help stay on track, I ask safety committee members to help communicate the needs for the last quarter of the year. Members will meet with each shift team to update them on any training needs. At times, they may even deliver training to individuals or to a team.

In November, the committee will also help create a list of required training and activities for the following year. This ensures fresh ideas are generated, so that we can plan some sweet activities!

There is nothing worse than the same old training every year; it may meet the requirements of the OSHA standards, but is painful to sit through and provides little value to employee safety.

Summary

- As you may have picked up by now, I am a super-fan of safety committees. They are a crucial part of your safety army, the pulse of the safety program, and can help you drive improvements.
- I encourage you to determine what ideas to implement from this chapter to help keep committee members engaged.
- And, most importantly, don't forget to reward them for all the awesome work they do.

At least one employee will undoubtedly ask, "When is enough, enough?" The answer is *never*.

HOURLY WORKFORCE ENGAGEMENT – WHEN IS ENOUGH, ENOUGH?

The safety committee isn't the only group that you need to motivate and engage. The hourly workforce is just as important when it comes to participation in the safety program. Employees typically need to know the "why" behind the "what" in order to get involved. Who would want to be inconvenienced by more documentation, participation, and engagement without knowing **why**?

At least one employee will undoubtedly ask, "When is enough, enough?" The answer is ***never***. Companies are constantly evolving and improving. An operations team is always looking for ways to reduce costs, improve throughput, and eliminate headcount. The quality team looks to reduce consumer complaints and eliminate deviations in the process. The safety team is no different.

We must constantly look for ways to reduce injuries as both workers and the operations process change. When the end goal shifts, it impacts all areas of the plant, including the safety program.

When either production or workload needs to increase, safety and quality are impacted.

Let's look at an example situation that many manufacturing companies face—cases of product out the door needs to increase over the next year. Companies don't typically think about how the safety of their employees is impacted when they ask for more, without providing more resources. When the staff stays the same and the hours in the day don't change (how would it?), then how is the team supposed to produce more output with the same input?

One simple answer—shortcuts. Finding ways to save time can come down to eliminating safety procedures such as locking out equipment, filling out a hot work permit, or putting on the required PPE. This is a terrible decision that affects the bottom line; however, it is rarely planned out ahead of time.

Simply taking the time to meet with the whole team can prevent injuries. One way to do this is scheduling a meeting with all stakeholders in your company or location. Operations, safety, quality, engineering, supply chain, etc. can meet to determine what the end result must be. If the goal is to produce 100 more cases of product per day, this gives us a starting point. Let's say it takes 30 minutes to make an additional 100 cases. The team will need to figure out how to save those 30 minutes from other tasks.

For example, if locking out the machine multiple times per day takes five minutes per occurrence, is there a way to reduce that down to three minutes per occurrence? Can lockout points be combined or relocated to eliminate the time it takes to walk to each one? If lubrication points are relocated outside the equipment, can that task be done while the machine is running rather than shutting it down and locking it out? Also, does each task have to be done once per day, or can the frequency be extended to every other day?

All too often, we do things because it has always been done that way! An example of changing procedure is the installation of an auto-lubrication unit on a case packer. Let's say the case packer was previously shut down for about an hour per shift for lubrication. To avoid this downtime, the plant installed an auto-lubrication unit for a reasonable cost. This positively impacted production by two hours per day, 365 days per year. To put those hours in perspective: When the case packer is down, it costs the company about $300 per hour, so this equates to over $200,000 per year gained!

Plus, there is added risk when employees handle chemicals, potentially drip grease or oil on the floor, climb on and around equipment, etc. All of these risks are eliminated by simply installing an auto-lubrication unit.

The safety of employees is rarely considered when determining how to save time, so it's critical that the safety team gets involved. For example, I worked with Rachel, an engineering employee, who developed and implemented capital projects at a manufacturing plant. There were the typical forms expected to be filled out to meet corporate requirements, but we developed a separate procedure to ensure all our bases were covered on new projects. Since we were ultimately responsible for the safety of our employees and any contractors onsite, it was critical to plan properly.

We implemented a pre-planning process that allowed us to discuss the project, determine the potential risks, and how to eliminate or address those risks. Performing a walkthrough of the area with the affected hourly team, helped us identify any issues prior to starting the project. Many times, the employees we spoke with had ideas about what we could do to improve the outcome. They also brought up concerns that we could address in the pre-planning phase of the project.

As part of one project, Rachel and I wanted to install new anchorage points as part of a personal fall arrest system. The area of the facility where we needed to install them is tricky to access; employees suggested we improve how to get to those anchorage points.

We took measurements, obtained quotes, and were then able to provide safe, accessible anchorage points for the employees. If it weren't for the interaction of the hourly team, we may have gotten it wrong. And who needs another barrier to performing work safely?

Gaining the trust of the hourly team takes work. It takes being visible and leading from the front lines. Simply pumping out safety policies, developing procedures, and doling out training will not result in a robust safety program with engaged hourly employees. An important way to maintain an engaged hourly workforce is by **asking questions and learning** what they do.

Don't just assume your new fancy-schmancy face shield is going to be loved by all. Ask employees to trial the face shield and provide feedback. Explain your expectations and reasons for wanting to change the process—whether it be cost, elimination of a newly discovered hazard, or a new corporate initiative. When you want to get feedback, go back to the employee. Don't expect them to come to you. Go to their work area, ask for feedback, and ask them to show you any barriers or reasons why it won't work.

As leaders in safety, we don't want employees to run away, hide, or grumble when we come around. We want them to embrace our visit by knowing that we are there as partners to work through challenges together.

I cannot stress enough that our hourly workforce are the ones we expect to do hard work, with less time, fewer resources, and under budget. We must support their efforts by establishing a collaborative work environment.

Now, with that being said, we are still not going to make everyone happy. At one point, I discovered that we had several bad fall arrest harnesses that needed to be replaced. Many were old and damaged, and the current model being used was discontinued. I communicated my findings with the maintenance team who wore these harnesses and told them we would conduct a trial with six new harnesses. I set up a station with the harnesses, asked the team to try each one, and fill out a voting ballot with their top choices.

I explained that we would settle on the harness that the majority of the team preferred, and it was important that each team member voted. I received nearly all of the voting ballots back and communicated the results. One employee was very upset with the results. He said that he felt his vote didn't count, and he wanted a different harness than the one the team had voted on.

I explained that some companies don't even ask for a team's input—they simply order new harnesses, and employees are expected to wear them. In this case, I wanted to give employees a voice, but knew that not everyone would agree. I expected everyone to wear the new style of harness and arranged to follow-up in a few weeks.

I followed up with the employee who was initially unhappy and was surprised by his new attitude. He told me that he was wrong. The new harness was of much better quality and was easier to put on than his other harness. He stated he was initially upset because he liked the comfort of his old harness, but now understood the reasons for changing. I thanked him for his comments and told him to keep me updated on any issues that might develop. He agreed.

Not every situation goes this smoothly. I had another employee, Drew, who was downright obstinate about a change to our work boot policy. We changed the policy to indicate that no part of a safety toe could be worn out and showing the steel or composite toe underneath. The company provided a 100% subsidy of safety shoes each year and felt the safety toe should not be compromised at any time.

Drew was not happy and made it verbally clear by scoffing at the new policy when it was explained in a team meeting. The employee's manager, Jason, observed Drew wearing a pair of safety-toe shoes that had a large part of the steel toe visible. Jason explained to Drew that he would need to get them replaced within the next week, as the new policy was effective immediately. Jason explained that he would help the employee navigate the safety shoe subsidy program, should he need assistance.

Drew was visibly and verbally frustrated. He was disciplined for his behavior and eventually terminated for non-compliance. So, not every situation is rainbows and unicorns! There are tough situations that require careful handling and unfortunately, disciplinary action up to and including termination.

Another important aspect of raising hourly employee engagement is to **give them ample time to participate**. If we truly value their participation and want their input, then build time into their day or week for them to perform their safety program duties.

Early in my career, I was promoted from the production area. At this point, I was able to operate almost all of the equipment in the facility. In my new role, I relieved other workers by running their equipment while they completed safety commitments. Sometimes it would take 10 minutes, sometimes 30 minutes. The team always appreciated the chance to step away and take the appropriate time to do their behavioral observation, audit, or inspection without having to hurry back. I loved the chance to support my team by allowing them to have meaningful participation. It also helped to prove that I would do what it takes to show them their contributions were valued.

Now, in some cases you may not be able to do this, or may not want to, and that's ok. I wanted to throw in this example, because it really helped me to connect with the hourly team. They appreciated the opportunity to step away and perform their safety tasks without rushing. I also got a chance to walk in their shoes—which always goes a long way!

If relieving someone isn't a possibility, then work some time into their schedule. If there is a changeover or some downtime coming up later in the week, then inform employees that they will be given time during that break in production to perform their safety observation, audit, or other safety-related tasks. Otherwise, let workers relieve each other as they would when covering for breaks or lunches.

Verify there is a system or method that works; don't let workers struggle to get all of their tasks done and then try to find time to perform their safety duties, too. Nothing is worse than waiting until the end of the month to find out that workers didn't have sufficient time, or weren't set up for success.

At another point in my career, an employee, Sean, had left our company to go work for another one, which was paying a dollar more per hour for the same work. He had been gone for about a month before he stopped by to talk with me. I have to say this was a bit odd since I didn't feel like we were close during the time he was employed. He said that while he was working at our company, he thought I was annoying. He thought that I was always milling around, observing, and trying to keep us safe. Actually, he found it irritating.

At this point, I wasn't sure why he came back to tell me this? Admittedly, I was a little offended! But he went on to say that at his new job, they planned to work on a caustic line. He told his boss that he hadn't received his lockout locks or training; his boss told him it wouldn't be necessary—just do the work by closing the valves. Sean said, "Don't we have a safety lady that comes out and asks if you are locked out?" His boss laughed and told him no.

Sean said he was a little shocked and became concerned about doing the job without locking out the valves, but he proceeded anyway. After a few hours, he suddenly felt something dripping down the back of his uniform, and it started to burn. Yep, you guessed it—caustic. He immediately went to the safety shower and rinsed off. Luckily, he only ended up with first degree burns. Someone had been done with their portion of the work and turned the valves back on.

He told me that he had learned to appreciate me and my persistence with lockout/tagout while underneath that safety shower. Sean also made it clear that a dollar more an hour wasn't worth the poor safety culture and risk of injury.

Summary

- Hourly employees are the heartbeat of a facility. They are my favorite part of my job. They keep the equipment running, process packages out the door, maintain equipment, and load and unload trucks. They perform observations, audits, inspections, and give life to the safety program. Keeping hourly workers engaged in the safety program is hard when they have so much going on already.

In future chapters, I'll give you more ideas on just what to do to keep them excited about safety!

The main thing I didn't know was how to overcome tragedy.

THAT WOULD NEVER HAPPEN HERE

At one point in my career, I started as an environmental, health and safety manager at a company that recently had a fatal workplace injury. The safety program was broken, but not as much as the employees. They lost faith in workplace safety. They were confused as to why it happened, and so many questions were unanswered. This was their friend, their coworker, and they missed him. I never met the man who died, but I can tell you that I thought about him every day after I took that job. I thought I knew a lot about workplace safety, but I'd never had a fatality in any of the facilities I worked in. **The main thing I didn't know was how to overcome tragedy.**

I was surprised to find that employees embraced safety at this facility. They followed written procedures, attended training, and had great attitudes about change. How could this facility still have injuries and especially a fatality?

The facility had developed a form of behavioral safety observations, but they were not being done properly. If you remember from my previous experience, I was a behavioral safety coordinator. My entire existence was built around observing employees work and reviewing the data! After reviewing the completed observations at my new job, I found that nearly all of the completed monthly observations were always safe.

How is it then that when I walk onto the production floor, I see risk everywhere? I determined a couple of potential reasons. Maybe employees weren't trained properly. They could just be filling out the form in the break room, not on the production floor, since we only tracked participation. Or maybe, they didn't know what risk looked like. I chose to believe the latter to give myself hope in teaching workers how to identify risk and determine the appropriate ways to eliminate it.

I decided to give the entire workforce a test. During our all-plant training, I set up 15 stations with mock at-risk situations and behaviors. I had the safety committee members pretend to perform certain tasks in an at-risk manner, such as cutting toward themselves with a utility knife, mixing chemicals with no goggles or gloves, using a portable ladder improperly, etc. I sent a dozen employees at a time through the stations and gave them 3 minutes to write down all the risks they observed.

I was surprised by the results. I had one employee tell me **he could only identify one risk**.

"Is that bad?" he asked.

"No," I replied, "we are just practicing."

I went through each at-risk behavior one by one and explained the associated risk. One employee said that he didn't know if goggles were required for mixing those chemicals. I explained that it wasn't about knowing the rules, but understanding risk.

"What looks risky about that particular task?" I asked. "I am not here to teach you the OSHA regulations, but I am here to help you identify risk so that we can make adjustments to our behavior."

I also try to use the family example. "Would you let your daughter or son mix those two chemicals without using goggles?"

That can be a reality check—of course they wouldn't!

I explained that when you observe someone doing something risky, just have a conversation about it. Why are you doing it that way? Could you wear goggles when mixing those chemicals? Did you know that particular chemical has sulfuric acid in it and can cause severe burns?

Ask for their commitment to do it differently and to find a solution that works for everyone. Identify any potential issues that might prevent someone from working safely. Do we stock chemical suits in size 4X that will fit that employee? If not, how do we go about stocking that size? Has anyone been notified that a change is needed?

I had so many employees speak to me after that day to talk about the exercise. One employee, Isabel, said she was embarrassed. She had previously been part of the safety committee and thought she was a good safety advocate. She was surprised at how much she didn't know. I reassured her that I had a plan to help employees identify and address behaviors and physical hazards in a more positive way. She went on to be one of the best identifiers of risks at that facility!

We did that same exercise again the following year to see if there was an improvement in our employees' ability to identify risks. This time they were excited to find the risks and challenge each other. After a year of training and monthly challenges, they were able to identify nearly all risks!

I wasn't at all surprised though, I must say. The previous year included so many opportunities for training, coaching, and learning from each other. I saw improvement even in employees who I was warned would be resistant. They were hungry to learn. I found that they were onboard as long as they had the right information and solid support for safety. At this point, I sensed we were developing a strong safety culture, and I wouldn't be the only one driving safety.

Slowly but surely, the team transformed. I would like to say I helped change the culture, but as I mentioned, it was already one that embraced safety; employees just didn't know what "good" looked like when it came to a workplace safety program.

After implementing the aforementioned training and activities, I noticed that workers started asking me a lot of questions and were requesting me to "come and look at this." I made it a point to go out on the production floor multiple times per day. Anytime they asked, I made it a priority to address their concerns.

One time, an employee, Brenda, was transferred to a new piece of equipment; I wasn't aware of the change. She came into my office to tell me that she had not yet received lockout/tagout training for her new piece of equipment; she would have to lockout the equipment later that day.

I was excited to hear that she knew she needed training, even if she could "figure it out" on her own. These small changes together signal success—when employees drive the program, you know you're making it work.

Now, in this particular case, we also identified a gap in our process. The operations team did not have a concise way to track who had lockout/tagout training on specific equipment. The operations and safety teams developed a training matrix to include all employees and each piece of equipment. As employees received training on a piece of equipment, it was now documented. Supervisors could use this training matrix when they transferred an employee to a new piece of equipment, promoted someone to a new position, or when calling in someone for overtime to help with a changeover.

I've shared how we were able to successfully educate our team even after the workplace fatality; now, I'd like to discuss the stress I felt when I began to address it. **When a serious workplace injury or fatality occurs, it is tricky to talk about the incident.** Do you bring it up? Do you acknowledge the incident and contributing factors? Do you tell new employees what happened? How do you know people's feelings toward the safety program?

My advice is to **talk about it and be sensitive**. Although I never met the man who tragically died that day, I acknowledge the incident. I discuss what we could have done differently, what we are doing differently now, and how we can prevent incidents such as those in the future. Some employees will not want you to talk about it, while some will be upset if you don't acknowledge it. Regardless, I find that discussing the incident with the utmost respect for the fatally injured worker is the only way to address the situation.

Explain your purpose of the discussion, which is strictly to prevent future incidents. No one wants to go home injured, and our goal is to make sure that our employees, visitors, vendors, and contractors are healthy and safe when working on our property. Period.

As you can imagine, change after tragedy can go two ways.

Employees may be ready for positive change due to the serious incident, or they may be royally mad at the company for failing to protect workers.

Typically, OSHA is involved in any serious injury or workplace fatality, so many facts about the incident become public knowledge. My suggestion is not to hide the information that is public; state the facts, explain the situation, and move on. I have found that being upfront and honest with the entire workforce is the only way to go. Prepare your notes, and stick to the script. **Employees don't need gory details; they need to know what happened, how it could have been prevented, and what action needs to be taken—by the whole team.**

Don't focus on your opinion or the opinion of others. If a citation is issued, it must be posted, so be honest with employees. Also, corrective action must be taken, so focus your efforts there. Get employees involved in the corrective action, and discuss it so that everyone has a chance to hear the same message.

Have you ever done an incident investigation where workers inform you that the hazard has "been like that" for days, or months? *What? Why didn't anyone say anything about it?*

At times, workers may have reported the hazard to their supervisor, but nothing was done. Other times, safety work orders are submitted, but never completed. And in other scenarios, no one takes the time to report the hazard at all. This can be challenging.

In one instance, I investigated a serious incident where an employee injured their arm in a piece of equipment. The employee was cleaning a roller on a machine that was operating. The roller caught the sponge and pulled the worker's arm into the machine.

When I talked to employees after the incident, they told me the truth; they all cleaned the machine the same way—while it was running.

When I asked why they couldn't do it while the machine was shutdown, they said that they have "always done it that way." The workers said no one ever questioned why they did it while it was running. They were trained to do it that way, and no one had identified that task as a risk.

In many industries, this way of thinking is pervasive. Shutting down equipment to perform routine tasks seems like a waste of time; management feels as though trained workers can perform these types of tasks with little to no risk, which is totally false. Yes, there are tasks that are inherently risky, regardless of proper PPE or training. But we still must look at removing risks, or at least reducing them down to the lowest possible and acceptable level.

For example, a worker could receive a paper cut when handling cardboard boxes, which may be an acceptable level of risk. However, if a worker receives a laceration requiring sutures for working with sharp metal, we can implement cut-resistant gloves to reduce the likelihood of a severe laceration.

Summary

- The work of a safety professional or safety leader is hard. You not only have to prevent injuries, but may also need to respond to difficult situations including serious injuries or fatalities.
- Workers, or even managers, may say "that would never

happen here," **but it can happen anywhere if the safety program is fractured.**

- **Focus on the facts, learn from mistakes, involve employees, and don't give up.** Remember not to hide information from employees; they need to know the "why" and how it is going to be different in the future.

I learned from different folks that I wasn't clear enough in my messaging. When I reminded workers about locking out, I wasn't giving them the "why." I do a better job of that now. When I approach workers that are locked out, I may ask them about their family. "Do you have kids?" "They would be proud of you knowing that you will come home safe today." At times, I throw in a story about someone who did not make it home safely, to drive the point. And they sometimes share stories with me, too, like my friend the millwright.

There is a big
difference
between
rewards and
incentives for
safe behaviors
and those
of at-risk
behaviors.

SHOW ME THE MONEY!

As I mentioned earlier, **there are many ways we can reward, recognize, or simply thank employees.** I love rewards; they are one of my favorite parts of working in safety!

There are so many different views on rewards and incentives, but I'll explain my viewpoint and give you lots of awesome examples of how rewards can drive positive behavior.

First, there is a big difference between rewards and incentives for safe behaviors and those of at-risk behaviors. Rewards and incentives for at-risk behaviors might be getting the job done quicker, earning a bonus on the number of units produced, or setting a production record. There is a ton of guidance from OSHA on ensuring employees are not incentivized for behaviors that can place workers at-risk or discourage them from reporting injuries, illnesses, or hazards.

We should never tell employees that they will get a steak dinner, a gift certificate, or a t-shirt if there are no injuries for a period of time. While those are desired outcomes, this type of incentive is shown to discourage workers from reporting when they are hurt. If workers don't get their steak dinner because Connor receives a laceration that requires stitches, Connor may not report the incident. The entire team will be ticked off at Connor, feel punished, and be deprived of the steak dinner if he reports his injury. Who wants to ruin the chance for a reward for their entire team?

Tokens

My suggestion is to always reward safe and expected behaviors. **One way to do this is with tokens, coins, company certificates, etc.** I have used wooden nickels that were personalized with the company logo and purchased in bulk through an online retailer. I prefer to use something tangible rather than an electronic system, but some programs may not allow that, so a points-system could also be used.

It is important to note that there are many ways to implement a safety reward program while ensuring there isn't a sense of entitlement. This can be a tough balance, but through my 20+ years of experience, I have successfully implemented this program at multiple facilities in different industries. Yes, even the millwrights were engaged and wanted to earn rewards!

Don't think of it as just another program to manage—keep an open mind and know that it works. I have worked with thousands of employees and proven that small, consistent rewards will improve not only your safety results, but will engage all levels of employees in the program. Also, have patience, as it will initially take some energy, excitement, and encouragement to get it off the ground.

It is important to note that I carried out this program at two, Voluntary Protection Program (VPP) Star sites, and it was highly successful. It was even mentioned in both certification audits as a best practice. It is so critical that we don't incentivize the wrong behaviors, but I promise if you follow the principles I outline in this chapter, you'll have a successful program, too.

Now, let's dive into the specifics to get your program going!

I will use the term "tokens" in this chapter, but just know that a "token" is whatever you want it to be, in whatever denomination you choose. Some facilities may require a metal-detectable token, where others may want to print and laminate some kind of token or certificate.

I started by ordering enough tokens so that I would not run out and cause an interruption in my program. For example, for a little over 100 employees, I ordered 3,000 wooden nickels (aka tokens) that had the company logo on one side and the denomination on the other. This allowed for some employees to save their tokens and for some to spend them right away.

The great thing about these custom, imprinted wooden nickels is that they cost only a few hundred bucks for 3,000 of them. Only hourly employees were eligible to earn the tokens; our salaried-exempt staff would hand them out.

Next, I ordered a glass display case to stock with treats; these treats were available for employees to purchase with their tokens. These cases are typically used to display clothing, trophies, etc., but they also worked perfectly for our purpose. Plus, they are also only a few hundred dollars, depending on the size.

I usually choose one that is about waist high by about five feet wide. They typically have glass shelves; you can display the items you want to stock for your program rewards, along with the token cost for each item. They also lock to ensure security. See picture on next page for an example:

I stocked my display case with candy, beef jerky, potato chips, and other snacks. I initially spent a few hundred dollars to fill the case and about $100-$200 each month to maintain a plentiful bounty of items. This expense may fluctuate based on the number of employees eligible for the program, and your budget.

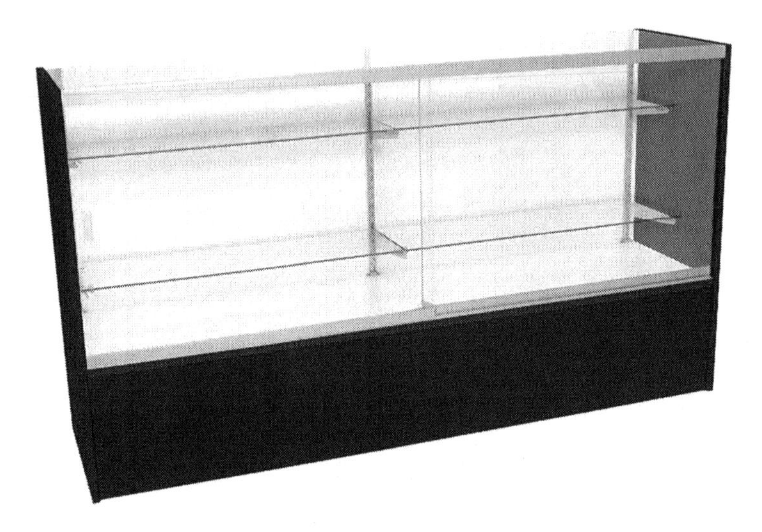

https://www.wayfair.com/keyword.php?keyword=glass+showcase+display

I also ordered company swag like hats, t-shirts, blankets, sweatshirts, travel mugs, lunchboxes, etc. that employees could only purchase with their tokens. I made it a point to order one-of-a-kind items, which could only be purchased with tokens that employees earned. The plant/operations managers made sure to congratulate employees when they saw workers wearing safety program swag.

The great thing about starting this program is that it can work with any budget. You can print out certificates instead of buying custom-printed tokens. You don't have to buy a display case; you can keep your items in a storage closet, and simply create a sign or PowerPoint slide that describes the items you have available for purchase. Don't worry about it being perfect at first; there may be a few bumps in the road, but it will be worth it.

Below is an example of imprinted tokens:

https://www.qualityimprint.com/products/lucky-wooden-nickelsq568411

After procuring the reward items, display case, and tokens, I created a matrix that outlined how employees could earn safety tokens. Managers and supervisors would hand out the tokens when employees were observed performing their work safely.

Now, this doesn't mean that every single time someone wears

the correct PPE, they should receive a token. It means that if a supervisor always sees Evan locking out correctly during a changeover, the supervisor would make contact with Evan, explain the safe behavior they observed and issue a token. **The purpose of the program is to regularly confirm the expected behavior and reward employees.**

I always explain that the reward list and items, earning potential, and token cost can change at any time. The program is fluid and depends on budgeting and participation.

Here's an example of how employees could earn tokens:

Safety Token Earning Power											
	Manager Recognition	Successful Answer to EHS Question	Valued Safety Participant	Manager Audit Compliance	Safety Committee Member Meeting Attendance	Completing a Quarterly Audit	Safety Challenge Winner				
Earning Power	1	1	1	1	2	3	5				
Award Levels											
Prizes	$1	$2	$5	$8	$10	$15	$20	$25	$50		
Cookies	X										
Candy	X										
Pringles		X									
Bagged Candy/Cookies		X									
Beef Jerky			X								
Small Gifts			X	X							
Company T-Shirt					X						
Company Travel Mug					X						
Company Hat/Visor					X	X					
Gift Cards					X		X				
Hoodie/Jacket								X	X		

After implementing the token program, I created a written program to outline the procedures and reward levels. We had several other established, safety reward programs to roll into this program.

For example, each lift truck was equipped with an impact alarm that would automatically activate if the lift truck made contact with an object. Previously, drivers would receive a gift card for having no impact alarms each quarter. With the new program, they would now instead receive tokens for not having any impacts.

Since our lift trucks were equipped with an automatic sensor that sent a message instantaneously, there was no concern about unreported impacts. Lift truck drivers loved the new program. Instead of getting another t-shirt or gift card they didn't want or need, they got tokens to spend how they chose.

This type of reward program can change the behavior of employees and encourage them to act safely—even when no one is looking.

When I first started with a new company as a safety manager, I felt that my role was one of discipline: to correct at-risk behaviors. I soon realized that the focus needed to be on pointing out what workers did right!

I would walk the production areas daily and talk with employees. When I first started my walks, I found that employees were nervous that I would point out something they were doing wrong. They would actually walk away to a different part of the production area when I came around.

If employees are only addressed when doing something wrong, they will simply try to avoid you and still perform that at-risk behavior when you're not around.

Although OSHA primarily discourages incentivizing certain behaviors (like not reporting injuries), encouraging safe behaviors is totally allowed! And...it works! It might be out of the ordinary or feel a little bit different at first, but you'll get the hang of it and see how your employees react.

In the example mentioned above, I knew something had to change; I had to get workers to **want** to show me the good things they do to keep themselves and others safe.

After getting the token program established and training employees on how they would be rewarded, behaviors and engagement immediately shifted.

Employees would now call me over to show how they had properly locked out, were using correct PPE, or to point out someone else who was working safely. Instead of walking in the other direction, they walked toward me.

This important shift in behavior helped me lead two facilities to receive VPP Star certification. One of the most important elements of the VPP is **management leadership and employee involvement.** How much better can it get when you have workers safely performing tasks and managers in turn rewarding those workers? Well, hang on, because there's more!

The program also encouraged supervisors and managers to recognize employees regularly for performing their duties safely. The goal for each manager and supervisor was to hand out at least five tokens per week. With about 20 supervisors and managers, that was a healthy goal; some leaders handed out many more. Hourly employees began asking me to reward other employees for their safe behaviors.

A specific example was when an employee wanted to reward Terry for always ensuring their safety gear was prepped and ready to go when sanitizing equipment with a potent chemical. Terry would go to the parts room, check out safety gear for both employees, and have it staged and ready once the time came to perform the sanitation. Employees began to find ways to reward others for supporting safety and making it easy to comply.

Another example was when an employee saw Simone stop to clean up a spill as she was walking to the lunchroom. Simone didn't create the spill but put out a cone and retrieved some paper towels to clean up the mess, thus preventing a potential injury. When I approached Simone to discuss the situation, she wasn't aware anyone saw her clean up the spill. I thanked her for making safety a priority, even when no one is watching.

Now, don't get me wrong; I have had a few employees in my tenure that were not enthusiastic about receiving tokens and thought it was childish. I remember a guy named John who was really not a fan of anything. When I implemented the program, he thought it was stupid; employees are paid to do a job, and safety is part of that job. Although I agreed, I explained that when employees do a great job, they are rewarded not with just a paycheck, but with a raise or bonus. The safety reward program also encourages positive behaviors at work. However, regardless of whether an employee does the bare minimum or goes above-and-beyond, they will still get paid. So, what incentive is there to perform the work safely? There are many, even beside pay raises or rewards.

Some employees want to perform their work safely so that they are not injured and can do all the things they want in their time away from work. Other employees want to work for a company for a long time and need to perform their work safely in order to do that. Others may simply not want to let their team down.

But often, employees still want to be recognized or rewarded for doing the right thing.

Although John wasn't a fan of the reward program at first, he eventually understood the intent and what the company was trying to achieve. He often earned tokens and shopped for those coveted one-of-a-kind items!

An important feature of the program was that employees would not lose their tokens for at-risk behaviors. Once they earned them, they were theirs to keep. My guidance to supervisors was that if they observed workers at-risk, they were to coach them and ask for their commitment to do the task safely in the future. If the employee agreed, they could still receive a token.

I once observed a worker on the production line not using gloves when handling corrugated material. I asked why he was not wearing gloves. He stated he had taken them off to do other tasks and forgot to put them back on. I explained the purpose of the gloves was to keep him from cutting his hands, even though the cut he could receive may be minor. I also explained that minor cuts can get infected and require medical attention. I asked the employee if he understood why we require gloves for that task, and he stated that he did. I then asked him if I could get his commitment to make a more conscious effort to wear gloves when handling corrugate. He stated that he would.

I then asked what he could do to make sure those task-specific gloves were available when he needed them. The employee told me that he would get another pair of gloves and keep them where he needed them. I told the employee that I appreciated him taking the time to find a safe solution, and that I would be back to check on him to confirm his commitment.

Later that same day, I checked on the employee; he was indeed wearing his gloves, so I rewarded him with a token and told him to keep up the good work! Whenever I see this same employee wearing his gloves, I give him a thumbs up and tell him "good job."

Another way you can drive safe behaviors is to talk about what employees are doing. At times, I observe employees performing work safely and then report it back to other managers. One time, I attended a leadership meeting. The other managers and I discussed an employee in the warehouse who would always turn off his lift truck when someone approached him. I asked a few of the managers to walk out to the driver later that day to speak to him about his safe behavior. As expected, the managers approached the driver, and he stopped his lift to turn it off. The managers commended the worker for his safe behavior and gave him a few tokens.

Later that day, the worker came in to talk to me. He said he had been a little nervous when he saw the managers coming toward him, and thought for sure he was in trouble! When they told him that he was doing a great job and wanted to reward him, he was pleasantly surprised and felt good about being recognized for his safe behavior. He thanked me for starting the program, and said he couldn't wait to spend his tokens.

One concern you may have is that this type of program could turn into an expectation or entitlement for employees. There are a few ways to explain this to workers. First, this may be a self-funding program. If we get the results we seek, then we will hand out more tokens and have lots of great swag for employees to buy. **Explain**

what the goals are and be clear. If the goal is to improve safety committee attendance or achieve 100% compliance with PPE, then explain that to employees.

Here were a few of my goals: to have at least 75% participation in monthly activities; to improve behavioral observations (this included reporting at-risk behaviors that I measured); and to ensure that safety work orders were completed within the number of days outlined in our policy. These were all measurable and communicated to the facility. Employees knew that in order to continue a token reward program, they needed to work together.

I have had a few employees point out their safe behaviors and want a token for doing the right thing. If this happens, I typically give the employee an assignment that allows them to earn a token. I ask them to perform a task or series of tasks that I need done, such as writing safety work orders, hanging signs on equipment, or performing an inspection.

Employees may have different reasons for requesting tokens. At times, I have found that workers simply love the program and need a few extra tokens to get the item they want. It isn't so much out of greed as it is out of excitement. I suggest redirecting their attention to how they can obtain a token or two, and explaining how the program works.

On the contrary, you may have employees who are just plain greedy or are looking for free and easy ways to obtain tokens. You will always have a few bad apples; don't get discouraged! There are always good people who just love getting rewarded for doing the right thing.

Scratch-Off Cards

Another cool way to get all staff involved is to include your managers and supervisors in a similar program. Since I couldn't have managers and supervisors handing out tokens *and* earning them, I created a salaried employee reward program. Let's face it; salaried employees are encouraged and motivated by rewards, too!

I ordered some customizable scratch-off cards online. These scratch-off cards can be printed to say anything you want and are simple to assemble. I printed each card with either "one token" or "two tokens," so that I could hand them out to our salaried staff.

Many times, these staff members go above and beyond to help the safety program, even with little or no recognition. You can determine whether the scratch-off cards are earned the same way as the tokens or differently.

For example, for completing their homework, I gave tokens to hourly safety committee members and scratch-off cards to the salaried staff. They absolutely loved it. Plus, it was cool to see our salaried staff all decked out in safety program swag. I even had an hourly employee who wanted to reward our warehouse manager for picking up pieces of wood from broken pallets. The hourly employee had been sweeping and cleaning all day but couldn't seem to get caught up with production. He said it made an impression on him that the manager cared enough to give them a hand to prevent an incident or injury. I gave the employee a few scratch-off cards to give to the warehouse manager; it made an impact on the manager as much as his actions had made an impact on the employee.

Summary

- This reward program is fairly easy to implement, but will take some work to manage. It's important to keep it fresh and exciting over time.
- I have found that having a focused monthly topic such as lockout tagout, confined spaces, or hot work helps to keep things new and engaging. Managers and supervisors can then go out and look for those positive behaviors to reward.
- You should also encourage the team to discuss who was rewarded and the details of their safe behavior. This can really confirm that the team is doing the right work.

Nothing is
as valuable
as talking
with
workers.

JUST ANOTHER FLAVOR OF THE MONTH

Some of the biggest challenges of a safety professional's career is how to get employees excited about workplace safety and how to keep them consistently involved. Over the last two decades, I have made this a priority and saw very positive results—not just for a successful, injury-free culture, but for morale, too.

In the beginning of my career, I was a super enthusiastic, often times annoying, safety professional who wanted to make a big impact on the safety program. I thought my smile and charm would be enough to get people to do what I wanted, but as it turned out it wasn't enough. Damn.

I took many safety and health classes and read so many regulations to improve my knowledge in workplace safety, but **nothing was as valuable as talking with workers.**

Employees don't know the regulatory requirements. They don't always know why the rules are in place. They also don't always know the rules or how to follow them. Over the years, I came up with several ideas to engage the workforce and get them to participate in the safety program. Having various ways for employees to be involved has really helped drive excitement around safety. As in previous chapters, there are always outliers to struggle with (those employees who could care less about participating in anything, especially workplace safety).

One of the first things I started was something I called the **"Safety Flavor of the Month"** challenge. Exactly how it sounds, it is a different safety challenge each month that focuses on a specific topic. A simple internet search can provide you with topic ideas, or you can focus on challenges within your own facility.

For example, during your inspections you find several lockout locks that are missing employee names, and hot work permits that are missing critical information; these issues would be perfect for a "Safety Flavor of the Month" challenge.

Each month, choose a topic such as lockout/tagout, confined spaces, hot work, or fall prevention, and provide a challenge for that topic. Place challenge paperwork or forms somewhere easily accessible for employees. Employees take a form, fill out the form or challenge, and turn it into the safety department by the deadline. I typically give my challenges a two-week deadline to allow plenty of time for employees to participate.

I usually give out three main prizes (five tokens) to random winners, which makes the stakes a little higher. I also put all the names of participants and winners on a board or monitor for all employees to see, along with a thank you message for their participation. Employees get a token just for participating; if they get any of the answers incorrect, I make a copy and add my comments to give back to the employee.

You don't want to discourage employees from participating by only giving tokens to those who get the answers correct. You want to correct any errors so that they can learn while participating!

Here are a few ideas for monthly challenges:

- **Confined Spaces.** Fill out a confined space permit with correct, incorrect, and missing information. Take several pictures of the completed, confined space permit and ask employees to circle the pictures with the correct information.
- **Safety Glasses.** Copy or create a QR code that employees can scan to watch a short video on safety glasses and their purpose. In addition to the QR code on the challenge form, have a few questions for the employees to answer about the video.
- **Lockout/Tagout.** One of my personal pet peeves, which can also be a company policy, is when employees don't have their full names on lockout locks. We have seven employees named John! This challenge is for employees to identify the requirements for locks and isolating equipment.
- **Hearing Protection.** This challenge took a little more time for employees to participate, but it was fun to watch. I took pictures of each of our hearing protectors in the facility and put those on one side of the challenge form. On the other side, I listed various noise reduction ratings (NRR), and employees had to match the hearing protector to the correct NRR. Needless to say, I found a lot of hearing protectors in the lunchroom as employees filled out their forms.
- **Hazard Communication.** Chemical safety is super important and is also one of OSHA's top-cited programs. This challenge includes a list of chemicals available in the facility, and their

related hazards. Employees must match the chemical to the hazard.

- **Safety Improvements.** This one took me a lot of time to prepare, but employees loved it; it helped me spread the word about improvements being made. Make a map of the facility with stars on it in five locations. In each of the five locations, put before-and-after pictures and a short story about what was corrected or addressed in that area. On their challenge form, workers must describe what had been corrected in that area.

  It was really cool to see people with their map going to other areas of the facility to find the answer. Employees said this was their favorite challenge and I did it again every six months or so to showcase some of the improvements we made. The cool thing about this challenge was it got employees to go to different areas of the plant and talk to their coworkers about safety. It also helped them get ideas about how we could implement the same corrective action in their area.

When I first started the "Safety Flavor of the Month," one of the managers came into my office complaining that employees were working together and sharing answers on the monthly challenges. When I walked into the lunchroom, I saw multiple people eating their lunch and talking about their answers. It actually made me really happy. Employees were sitting around talking about safety on their lunch break—how awesome is that?! What is the alternative? Employees sitting around NOT talking about safety.

Also, I found that my most stubborn and grumpy employees participated. I made it a point to ask if they saw the challenge was posted and that the deadline was nearing. At times, I would get a grunt or "yeah, whatever," but I never stopped asking them to participate. When I did get a completed challenge form from those employees, I made it a point to call it out.

Obviously, a program like this is so much easier in a small facility; so, **if you have several hundred or thousands of employees, then focus on a quarterly or annual program rather than monthly.**

Conducting these types of challenges and exercises allow you to identify weaknesses and strengths in your safety program. Results from these activities can tell you where you need to focus your efforts.

If while doing the lockout/tagout challenge you see that most people got the answers wrong, then retraining is necessary. If most everyone found the incorrect or missing information on the confined space permits, then you can focus your efforts elsewhere.

One thing you may find is that **employees get excited about games, challenges, and competitions.** Many times, employees would ask me when the next "Safety Flavor of the Month" challenge would be posted. Although I tried to post it on the first day of the month, at times I had conflicting priorities, causing it to be a day or so delayed.

I would often ask safety committee members to help with topics and challenges, so that we could be prepared a few months in advance. It was exciting that employees were anxious for the next challenge!

The objective of these challenges is to get employee involvement in the safety program. Aim to make the challenges fun, light-hearted, or funny to pique their interest. Of course, we want to teach them something, too, but the overall focus should be getting workers to participate. Think about how popular the daily or weekly crossword puzzles were in the newspaper; customers couldn't wait until the next one came out. Rather than just reading the news, which was the purpose of the newspaper, readers would routinely complete the crossword puzzle as part of their daily or weekly ritual.

Summary

- Ultimately, employees will be more engaged, and either learn more about the activity topic you choose or confirm that they already know the material.
- Employee engagement and participation is critical to the success of the safety program and safety culture. You may have a few workers that aren't interested at first, but over time, you'll get their participation and have a little fun doing it!

Flavor of the Month Challenge
Turn in by October 21st!

Name:____

Watch the following YouTube video on impact resistant eyewear and answer the questions.

https://www.youtube.com/watch?v=UBZhP3mkFs4

1. Impact resistant eyewear has what ANSI rating?
    a. Z87.1
    b. Z100.2
    c. 96.5
    d. 98.5

2. How fast is the ¼" ball traveling in the first test?
    a. 100 mph
    b. 101 mph
    c. 102 mph
    d. 103 mph

3. What caliber projectile is fired at the lens in the military ballistic impact test?
    a. 10 caliber
    b. 15 caliber
    c. 20 caliber
    d. 25 caliber

4. How fast is the military ballistic impact test projectile traveling?
    a. 102 mph
    b. 220 mph
    c. 330 mph
    d. 440 mph

5. In the last test comparing the military rated versus the ANSI rated eye protection, wha were the results?
    a. The ANSI rated eyewear performed equally to the military rated eyewear.
    b. The military rated eyewear failed.
    c. The military rated eyewear were superior.
    d. All of the above.

Safety Flavor of the Month Challenge!

July's SFOTM is Lockout. Answer the following questions about lockout and turn in your completed form. You can scan it, email it, put it in my mailbox, hand it to me, etc.! Do this by Friday, August 7th!

1. What are the minimum requirements for labeling your lockout lock?

____

____

2. Where should you put your key after you have locked out equipment?

____

____

3. What is the last step in lockout before you can safely work on equipment?

____

____

Keep a training matrix for the electrical, lockout, and confined space programs.

NO, YOU CAN'T JUST SKIP TO THE TEST

Most employees will tell you they hate receiving or attending safety training. It is boring, repetitive, and takes a ton of time. In my career I have encountered so many safety professionals that implement a computer-based training program where employees receive 100% of their training. This makes me crazy! Although easy, I feel it completely sucks! That's what this book is all about—making workplace safety NOT suck.

Let's look at how to stay organized and focus on the requirements, and then at what employees must know to do their job safely.

First and foremost, **I create a training matrix** each year, which includes all employees (template available at the end of this chapter and at LisaKnowsSafety.com). I create several tabs within a spreadsheet for each department, and then add the employees for each. At the top, I add the topics that must be trained due to regulatory requirements. I then add any other topics that we need to train on for that year.

I consider this a living document (one that gets updated regularly); so, it's important that if many people use it, they are using the most current version. I like to add a time/date stamp to ensure that if a copy is printed, they can see the date. This prevents confusion for managers and supervisors, as without the date stamp, they sometimes think a lot of workers have not completed their training.

I prefer to keep computer training to no more than 50%-60% of the total safety and health training. Employees will find ways to "get through" the computer-based training by taking it multiple times or guessing. I will typically use a computer-based training "test" after I educate workers on the topic. Plus, there is nothing like **live training** where someone can see an example, watch a video, or hear a story firsthand.

Here are some examples of training you can do, along with a mixture of videos and computer-based training:

- **Emergency Evacuation.** Find a video on the internet such as the one about the Station Nightclub fire in Rhode Island that killed 100 people. Show clips from the video, and then talk about the importance of keeping exits clear, maintaining appropriate occupancies, or general fire safety. This tragic accident makes for an excellent training tool to prevent future deaths.
- **Lockout/Tagout & Energy Control.** Show a video, such as the one regarding the Bacardi® Rum factory death of a temporary worker on his first day. Explain why proper training on the first day is just as important, if not more so, as annual refreshers regarding energy control. Discuss ways to prevent these types of injuries, and how this worker's family was affected by this terrible incident.

- **Fall Arrest.** Using a tape measure, cones or other items, show employees how safe fall distances are calculated. Pictures and videos are also available on the internet to help enhance the visual. When employees realize just how far 18+ feet is when shown in a room, their reaction speaks for itself.
- **Fire Extinguishers.** Teaching employees how to use extinguishers may be required, but how you do so, isn't specified. I prefer doing live exercises when possible, where each employee gets an opportunity to use an extinguisher. I partner with our fire protection company to hold the training and have them onsite to refill dry chemical extinguishers when needed. This typically costs $300-$400 a year for their assistance and to recharge extinguishers.

  Years ago, I used to have a propane-powered fire box but found it to be dangerous and cumbersome to set up. Now, I simply have employees fight a simulated fire by printing out pictures of fire and pasting them to an item. A fun way to do this is changing up the item that is "on fire" each year. At thrift stores or online, you can find a cheap child's playhouse to paste pictures of fire to and have employees attempt to extinguish the fire. Although it is a simulated exercise, employees get the feeling of how to properly operate an extinguisher.

  During this time of year, I've also had employees bring in their personal, dry chemical, rechargeable fire extinguishers from home, and the company pays to recharge them while they are in the training. This is a great way to give back to our employees, by ensuring they have a safe, fully charged fire extinguisher at home.

- **Scaffolding.** Have qualified scaffolding employees set up some scaffolding with errors; make sure you tag it out and label it for training purposes only. Have employees inspect the scaffolding for errors or omissions to see if they can correctly identify the issues. Share a story and pictures, such as the incident in Egypt where three workers died when scaffolding failed due to improper setup.

To me, training is very important and must be value-added. If we assign lockout/tagout authorized user training to everyone, but not everyone is authorized, then it really frustrates the team. If we develop authorized and affected user training, then it makes more sense. Although it takes more work on our part upfront, it drives engagement for employees; this way they only receive the training they need.

Think about some of the comments you may have heard over the years. I have often heard complaints on workers receiving training for topics that did not affect them. It is easy to just lump everyone into the same category; trust me when I say that I have done this before, solely because it was easier on me. It will not get you where you want, or need, to be to build an enviable safety culture.

When employees see that you take the time to ensure they receive proper training, they have more respect for you and the safety program. What drives participation further is by presenting training in an engaged format, such as face-to-face or instructor-led; and with awesome accompaniments such as current/interesting videos or other examples. By creating the training matrix, you can easily identify which employees, in each department, require training in each topic.

I also tend to keep a separate matrix for the electrical, lockout, and confined space programs. For the electrical safety program, I have a list of qualified workers, their training dates, and annual company recertifications listed in the matrix. It helps me to keep track of the workers that are qualified to work on electrical equipment, along with when their training or reviews are due. If you have company-specific requirements or want to add further information, such as annual observations to comply with the National Fire Protection Association (NFPA) 70E, having multiple matrices is a great way to ensure you are meeting the requirements.

For lockout/tagout, the matrix has tabs for each department and their respective employees. All lockout/tagout procedures are listed across the top; once the employee has been trained on that procedure, an X is placed in the box to indicate training is completed. This is also a great way for supervisors to see who is already trained when a replacement worker is needed for a change-over or repair. They can simply refer to the list. It also helps when someone is being promoted or transferred to another department. Many times, teams are short-handed and need to pull someone from another department; supervisors can refer to the lockout/tagout matrix to see who has already been trained, then bring them over to help out.

For confined spaces, I maintain a list of each employee that has been trained to be an entrant, attendant, entry supervisor, or rescue team member. I have a column for each person, the task or job, and the dates they received the training. It helps me keep track of new employees that join the company and need training—I simply add them to the matrix and document the date they were trained. This matrix is also available to the supervisors who can see who is currently trained for all related tasks for confined spaces in the case of a needed entry.

Another piece of advice I would like to offer is to **have someone conduct training that knows the subject well and who has actually done the job.** Nothing is worse than hiring a consultant that only knows the regulatory requirements. For example, I have met many safety professionals and consultants that teach topics like CPR but have never administered it to a human being. I insist on bringing in someone that has experienced giving someone CPR to fully explain the impact of the training. Yes, it can be expensive; but, on a scale of importance, CPR is a lifesaving skill which should be given our full resources. It is simply not as impactful or useful to learn the skills from a book or inadequate teacher.

If you haven't participated in or conducted a confined space entry, don't try to do the training without help. Get out there and observe an entry. Talk to workers; find out what works efficiently as well as what needs further attention or training. The same with lockout/tagout, or any other topic. Learn the material first-hand so that you are an educated, experienced trainer.

Your employees must know that you understand the risks and potential barriers to compliance; this is critical to employee engagement. Would you teach someone how to drive a car, having never driven one yourself? The answer should be NO! Learn and practice the material, before conducting training.

While developing your training, determine which team or group will be attending and involve them in the material or class. For example, if you will be presenting confined space training, take some pictures during an entry at your facility to include in the training. Ask employees for their thoughts on the top three important aspects of a confined space entry, and **add those thoughts or quotes to your curriculum.** Employees will better connect with the course material when they see their names and quotes within the training. When others see their coworkers' names and quotes, it helps them to connect as well.

I also love to use props or equipment in my instructor-led/live training. Nothing is more impactful than bringing the confined space, four-gas detector; fall arrest harness; self-retracting lifeline; or other relevant equipment to the training. **Listening to someone lecture without any props is boring!** Get creative and implement equipment that employees may want to see or interact with.

Once, I brought in our newest, self-retracting lifeline, which had a rescue feature. If the lifeline was placed in rescue mode and a fall was arrested, the lifeline would then lower the worker slowly to the ground. Obviously, this is a specialized piece of equipment that can't be used everywhere (particularly over dangerous equipment), but would help the team when performing certain work. Employees were really excited about our commitment to reducing injury potential should a person fall, and end up hanging for a period of time until help arrived.

Another way you can use equipment in training is by bringing an automated external defibrillator (AED). Hearing the AED guide users how to properly utilize the machine can calm and reassure workers.

Another super fun way to engage workers is to have prizes or tokens for training participation. This could be for workers who participate in discussion, score a certain percentage on a related quiz, etc. I enjoy giving out tokens, but I also know teams get excited about food, candy, tools, and company swag like hats and shirts. **Determine what motivates your teams.** Working with a lot of millwrights and maintenance guys can be tough, but I have found that they love to bring candy and treats home to their kids!

I love to do training around Easter and Christmas, when employees can stock up on treats for baskets and stockings. Of course, they also enjoy goodies like beef jerky and BBQ seasonings. Company-logoed items such as shirts, hats, lunch boxes, thermoses, water bottles, backpacks, or tools work well, too. Gift cards are also an awesome reward if allowed by company policy; even a $10 gift card for a local fast food place is a great way to show appreciation and drive involvement.

Summary

- Safety training can really suck. Think about some of the ideas I mentioned in this chapter and how you can liven up your team's safety training. Can you bring props to your next training session? How about utilizing a captivating, true story or video to catch their attention?
- Remember from previous chapters, we want to have an event or discussion that will give workers something to remember and connect with. Will the team be talking about your awesome training in the lunchroom? Or will it be forgotten? The choice is yours.

Training Matrix Template

Employee Name	Department/Position	Training Topics											

Unlike the
"Safety Flavor of
the Month," the
"Safety Lookout"
challenge
focuses on
regulatory
requirements.

LOOK OUT!

After discovering that many employees didn't know why they had to wear chemical gloves, or why conveyors needed to be guarded, I worked with a safety committee member to create another type of challenge that I call the **"Safety Lookout"** challenge. Unlike the "Safety Flavor of the Month," **this challenge focuses on regulatory requirements.**

As I mentioned previously, the "Safety Flavor of the Month" challenge ran for a period of two weeks each month. To build on each topic of the month, the "Safety Lookout" challenge focuses on explaining the "why" behind the "what." We focus on teaching employees both what they have to do and why they have to do it. This isn't so that they can simply recite the regulations. They need to understand that these rules are in place to protect them, as well as to provide a level of insurance for their personal safety.

For the "Safety Lookout" challenge, I place a three-ring binder at each workstation, which includes information on that month's safety topic. The binders make it easy for employees to complete the challenges while at their workstation. All answers necessary to complete the challenge are included in the binder. Although this takes a bit of time to set up, the same information can be reused for future challenges.

Using a single document or slide, copy information from a regulatory reference and add pictures. Laminate the information, or put it in a sheet protector to add to each binder. Create a form with the same information where employees have to fill in the blanks with the missing (critical) facts. Don't forget to keep all submitted forms to track each employee's participation.

This challenge educates workers on the regulatory requirements and also gives them a chance to earn tokens or prizes. Although this seems very similar to the "Safety Flavor of the Month" challenge, I keep the "Safety Flavor of the Month" light-hearted and funny; I focus on the regulatory requirements for the "Safety Lookout."

I have found that once employees are educated, they are less likely to think it is "Lisa's Rule," or something I made up. This is essential when you are trying to build a culture where employees are knowledgeable, trained safety leaders—you need them to believe what you're saying!

Here are a few examples of "Safety Lookout" challenges:

- **General Industry Standard on Fall Protection.** The information that goes into the binder includes this excerpt from the OSHA regulation 1910.28(b)(3)(ii): "Each employee is protected from tripping into or stepping into or through any hole that is less than 4 feet (1.2 m) above a lower level by covers or guardrail systems."
  - » The challenge form states: 1910.28(b)(3)(ii) Each employee is protected from tripping into or stepping into or through any hole that is less than _____ feet (____ m) above a lower level by _________ or _____________ systems.

- **General Industry Standard on Abrasive Wheel Machinery.** The information that goes into the binder includes this excerpt from the OSHA regulation 1910.215(a)(4): "Work rests. On offhand grinding machines, work rests shall be used to support the work. They shall be of rigid construction and designed to be adjustable to compensate for wheel wear. Work rests shall be kept adjusted closely to the wheel with a maximum opening of one-eighth inch to prevent the work from being jammed between the wheel and the rest, which may cause wheel breakage. The work rest shall be securely clamped after each adjustment. The adjustment shall not be made with the wheel in motion."
  - » The challenge form states: 1910.215(a)(4) Work rests. On offhand grinding machines, work rests shall be used to support the work. They shall be of __________ construction and designed to be adjustable to compensate for wheel wear. Work rests shall be kept adjusted ________ to the wheel with a maximum opening of _________-_______________ inch to prevent the work from being jammed between the wheel and the rest, which may cause wheel breakage. The work rest shall be securely _______________ after each adjustment. The adjustment shall not be made with the wheel in motion.
- **General Industry Standard on the Control of Hazardous Energy (lockout/tagout).** The information that goes into the binder includes this excerpt from the OSHA regulation 1910.147(a)(2)(iii): "This standard does not apply to the following: 1910.147(a)(2)(iii)(A) Work on cord and plug connected electric equipment for which exposure to the hazards of unexpected energization

or start up of the equipment is controlled by the unplugging of the equipment from the energy source and by the plug being under the exclusive control of the employee performing the servicing or maintenance."

» The challenge form states: 1910.147(a)(2)(iii) This standard does not apply to the following: 1910.147(a)(2)(iii)(A) Work on cord and plug connected electric equipment for which exposure to the hazards of ________________ energization or start up of the equipment is controlled by the ____________ of the equipment from the energy source and by the plug being under the ____________ control of the employee performing the servicing or maintenance.

Summary

- All of these challenges and activities are meant to engage employees in some portion of the safety program. The activities are not mandatory, making it easy to decipher who is participating and the level of engagement at your facility. If you're not getting a lot of participation, talk to employees. What are the barriers?
- At one point, I was not printing enough forms; when employees finally had time to stop and pick one up, they would already be gone! I learned quickly to print more and have a master copy laminated for the supervisors, just in case they were quickly depleted.
- Don't be discouraged if your employees don't participate at first. It may take time to get everyone to regularly fill out the "Safety Flavor of the Month" or "Safety Lookout"

challenges. Typically, I found that at least 60%-70% of the hourly team would participate routinely. Some employees would forget to participate at times, but others never missed a month! I even had a few safety committee members like Aileen, who would make copies for her entire team. She wanted to ensure that each team member had the chance to participate.

- When I first started these challenges, I communicated what my intentions were—to gain further engagement in the safety program. I told the teams that I wanted to gauge where we were regarding information retention and participation.
- And like I mentioned, if I failed to get the challenge posted on time—boy, did I hear about it! Employees were anxious to earn their tokens and have some fun, too.

Document
everything!

YOU CAN'T TELL OSHA YOUR DOG ATE IT

After many years of building programs, addressing hazards, and writing policies I have come to an important conclusion—**document everything!**

Whether you want to prove that you're proactive, or just want to review how much you're accomplishing each day, it's important to document everything.

Early in my career, I had an interest in participating in one of OSHA's cooperative programs (I will discuss these programs in another chapter). I learned early on from other safety professionals that in order to *show* OSHA that you are doing something proactive, you better have proof. If you tell a regulatory agency that you perform monthly inspections on your fire suppression system or that you train workers on lockout/tagout, you must have proof that you indeed do these things.

The same goes for employee involvement. How do you prove that employees report hazards, participate in the safety committee, and are engaged? You must have documentation. **If you can't produce proof, you can't tell OSHA your dog ate it!**

In previous chapters, I discussed various ideas to get employees to be excited, engaged, and to participate in the safety program. So, the next big question is—**how should you document participation?** And what value does it bring?

It's easy to document activities like the "Safety Flavor of the Month" and "Safety Lookout" challenges. I simply create file folders for each employee; whenever they participate in an activity, I record it in their file. I provide a report at the end of each year to the facility leadership team; the report includes the total number of activities that each employee participated in throughout the year. It's a great way for managers and supervisors to see how frequently each of their employees participated. I have used this information to recommend someone for a promotion or raise, and also to be part of the safety committee moving forward.

As a bonus for safety committee members, I tally all homework completed within the year, and reward them with the respective number of tokens. What a super motivator to get them to finish homework!

Another suggestion I have for documentation is regarding the safety committee. I always have an **agenda prepared with all topics covered/to be covered,** to ensure we stay on task (template available in this chapter and on LisaKnowsSafety.com). It's easier to keep the committee engaged if they have this agenda; it allows them to see how many topics still need to be reviewed.

At the end of every safety committee meeting, I host a roundtable in which committee members can bring up any concerns, questions, or issues. In the meeting minutes, I document who was in attendance and who brought up a discussion point at the roundtable. This is also a good way to show who is attending and participating in safety committee meetings. Since I started documentation, many more committee members come prepared to meetings with topics or issues. If they don't have a safety issue or concern, I ask that they share an instance where they helped someone with their personal safety. So many great stories have been shared, and you can observe the engagement of committee members by their head nodding and agreement; it is so great to see.

Besides participation, **training documentation is super critical and goes a long way with auditors.** If you conduct computer-based training, ensure you have a copy of the material printed out (or easily printable). File or scan the material with a copy of the sign-in sheet to easily prove that training was completed with specific employees. Some regulatory requirements may also require the name or signature of the trainer (or person who created/assigned the training), so be sure to do your research on this. And of course—don't forget to update your training matrix!

Does your company have leadership meetings, safety work order reviews, or contractor safety reviews? Do you always start meetings with a safety discussion? How do you prove that any of these activities are taking place?

For example, if every meeting starts with a safety review, how do you prove it? A documented agenda can be posted on the wall for the team to review at the start of every meeting. When employees are asked if each meeting starts with safety, they can easily confirm what is on your agenda.

Do you conduct a weekly or monthly safety work order review? How is it documented? Who attends? A great way to ensure you have documentation of these meetings is to utilize a sign-in sheet, accompanied by a copy of what you reviewed. For example, at a weekly safety work order review, a sign-in sheet can be circulated to document who is in attendance. A copy of the safety work orders reviewed is attached to the sign-in sheet and filed. This proves that not only are we reviewing safety work orders weekly, but that different levels of employees are attending (managers, supervisors, and hourly employees). Another reason this documentation is great is that it shows that the team doesn't review the same work orders over and over; hazards are addressed in a timely manner. Copies of safety work orders completed in the previous month are also posted for employees to review the completed work orders.

I also document **attendance and agenda items at meetings like capital project reviews or maintenance outage reviews.** Many times, especially when applying for one of OSHA's cooperative programs, you must include discussions and planning for projects, maintenance, and non-routine work. I send around a sign-in sheet to take attendance at the meeting. This isn't to prove who missed the meeting! It is to show the different levels of employees that are engaged in the process. You may have maintenance mechanics, managers, quality technicians, and/or contractors attending these meetings. The discussion points or agenda items really help to document the potential safety issues that may be discovered during the project or outage. Some really great questions are asked during these meetings, which can help us avoid disaster. Recording all of these details is an excellent way to show an inspector or auditor that many workers of varying experience attend these meetings to ensure the company addresses all potential risks.

My biggest piece of advice for safety professionals is: **prove what**

you do. When you are buying a car or home, you must provide documentation such as proof of income, proof of last year's taxes, and/or current mortgage or rent payment. They do this because they want proof! The banks want to verify that you indeed earn a certain amount of money to qualify for the loan. The same goes for training, attendance, participation, etc. We want to be able to prove that we are doing the things we say we are.

Documenting your actions in a timely fashion can prevent huge fines from regulatory agencies and can help in the case of disciplinary action as well. If any employee is found to be in violation of a safety rule, we would likely turn to their training records or other documentation to prove that they did in fact already understand the related expectations to avoid a violation.

I can think of two, very specific issues where documentation played a significant role in whether someone received disciplinary action or not. First, I discovered an employee had not worn his electrical protective clothing when performing electrical work. I reviewed the training records and found that he had attended the training. I then reviewed the inspection records, which required employees to inspect their electrical safety gear every six months; he had indeed conducted his inspection. Our company also required an annual review with each electrically qualified worker to ensure they understood the requirements of their job, the associated protective gear, and electrical safety rules. He had received this review as well and had signed off that he understood the expectations.

Because we had conducted the training and reviews and had documented our steps, we were able to apply the appropriate level of discipline for this worker.

As another example, a supervisor had relocated an employee to another department during their shift, to cover an absence. The employee did not properly lockout a piece of equipment, and another employee immediately stopped the work after discovering the potential risk. In this case, we had not conducted training for the employee, so of course, it was not documented. Luckily, no one was hurt, but we discovered a gap in our training that we were able to address promptly. This serves as a good reminder of how important it is to not only conduct the training, but to document it as well.

Have you ever heard a supervisor or manager say that an employee is a poor performer after they get hurt? Now, they want you to do something about it! Great—the opposite of proactive; let's wait for an employee to get hurt, and then attempt to discipline them.

Using documentation to show performance is another way to help managers and supervisors address issues **before** someone gets hurt. If your company expects employees to be involved in the safety program, then documentation will help prove that.

I once had an employee tell me that his team on night shift was not getting a lot of tokens. I asked the employee if he had taken advantage of the many offerings at his disposal to earn tokens, such as the "Safety Flavor of the Month," "Safety Lookout" or safety committee participation. The employee stated that they didn't have time to do those activities and that he was also unaware he could join the safety committee. I explained that he could get what he wanted (more tokens) if he simply participated in the different activities we offered. He scoffed at the notion that he would have to do something to earn the tokens. I told him that I would be happy to come in early or stay late in order to observe employees during the night shift, and provide tokens for safe behaviors—after he completed the activities available to him.

I also explained that any employee at any time could join the safety committee, and that I would send him an invite. Needless to say, he not only didn't do any of the activities, but he didn't show up at the next safety committee meeting. I wasn't at all surprised, but this type of behavior really shows you who is solely interested in their own success.

Later, the same employee was found to be operating a lift truck with their seatbelt clasped behind them—a major violation at our facility, as the lift truck will not operate without the seatbelt clasped. The department manager asked for my records of participation and, unsurprisingly, he had not participated in any of the voluntary/supplementary safety activities during his employment with us. He had indeed attended lift truck training, passed the written exam, and passed the hands-on training—all of which were documented. The department manager felt as though we gave the employee multiple chances to be part of his own safety success, but yet he still failed to be proactive and to participate.

Summary

- Our overall goal is to ensure employees are engaged in the safety program, not just going through the motions. Any company can have a mediocre safety culture. If you want something different, create something different—a safety culture of participation, engagement, and high expectations.

This will yield much better results. Plus, employees feel proud to work for a company that doesn't just talk about safety, but implements it creatively with a purpose!

Safety Committee Agenda Template

SAFETY COMMITTEE AGENDA COMPANY LOGO

Meeting date | time | Meeting location

Type of meeting	Committee Meeting
Facilitator	

AGENDA TOPICS

Agenda topic *[Topic]* |

Discussion items

Agenda topic *[Topic]* | |

Discussion items

Agenda topic *[Topic]* |

Discussion items

Agenda topic *[Topic]* |

Discussion items

Agenda topic *[Topic]* |

Discussion items

Documented action plans are necessary and the key to a successful safety project or improvement plan.

ACTION PLANS – ARE THEY REALLY NEEDED?

Most companies and departments have action plans. In fact, they are vital to achieving goals and profiting; however, implementing action plans is not easy. In this chapter, we'll dive into why **documented action plans are necessary and key to a successful safety project or improvement plan.**

I started a job as a safety professional in a manufacturing facility with a poor safety record. On my first day, I met with my new boss. He gave me an overview of the safety performance and explained his expectations. He handed me a list of what he thought needed to be done to fix the broken safety program. I looked at the very long list and thought it would have been nice to get this during my interview!

He asked me to bring the list and meet with him each week, so that he could get a progress update. Great. So, off I went to audit, investigate, gather intel, talk to employees, take pictures, review systems, and cross things off the list.

When it came time to meet with my new boss the following week, I wasn't thrilled. He asked me where the list was; I told him that I threw it away. He was stunned. He sat there staring at me with his mouth partially open. I then pulled out my own list of what was **actually** wrong with the safety program. I explained that through my own evaluation, I found the situation was much different than he thought.

For example, one of the items on his list was to hold employees accountable for lockout/tagout violations. Through my interviews and observations, some employees were never issued locks and were never trained how to use them. How could I hold employees accountable when they were never provided the tools to safely perform their work? We had not set them up for success.

To develop an action plan, you first need to know what needs to be fixed. What is the problem you're trying to solve? What barriers do you have? What systems are you missing? For example, if I want employees to report hazards, how will they do it? Will they use an existing electronic system? Do they know how to use it? If an electronic method is not available, will they report hazards on a piece of paper? How will the hazards be tracked? How will we communicate the status of work to employees?

For each potential action, there must be a plan. Sounds reasonable, right? Ugh, it can be such a pain to document and plan everything! To make it easier, take care of each item in order. Let's use the example from above regarding the reporting of hazards. My first goal is to have employees report hazards. My actions are to teach them how to report the hazards using the electronic tracking system, and then correct or address each hazard. There are a few steps that I may need to take such as procure software, if one doesn't exist, that will help manage the hazards that are identified. I may also need to identify potential hurdles such as the ease of reporting hazards using the current system. Each item deserves attention and should be added to your action plan.

The great thing about an action plan is that you can see how far you've come over time. It is extremely rewarding to see so many small actions completed throughout the process!

Again, think about a weight-loss plan—you celebrate each small victory on your journey to lose weight; and reaching your goal weight is a cumulative success.

I use a standard action plan/action item tracker (included at the end of this chapter and at LisaKnowsSafety.com). The main reason I use an action plan is to ensure that I don't lose sight of all possible actions to take and the deadlines for each one. I would also like to mention that it is really important to **not take on too many actions at one time.** I usually only start with two or three actions, and track those to completion. Now, if things are going well, then I may start adding more actions; but, if there are 20 things to do, then it becomes overwhelming, time consuming, and difficult to manage—everything you don't want.

Let's go back to the reporting of hazards and create a detailed action plan. This action plan will focus on developing a system for reporting and tracking safety hazards through completion. Sometimes an action plan can last a month and sometimes a year, so **determine your targeted timeframe.** In this case, I am going to set my target at six months. And of course, if you need to extend your timeframe, just adjust your action plan dates. The purpose of the date is to ensure your team or boss understands when the plan will be fully implemented.

Now that we know the purpose of the action plan, we need to

determine the first few actions. Let's say that the first thing we need to do is review the current system in use. Who will be involved in the review, and what are we looking for? For this exercise, I'll create a cross-functional team of safety committee members, maintenance technicians, and managers. The team should be limited to 5-7 people, to keep everyone on task. They will look at what works in our current system and what doesn't. We should end up with a list of pros and cons of the current system, allowing us to determine what we need in a new system.

Make sure to document who is in charge or responsible for each action, and the expected completion date (ideally by the next meeting). If everyone is expected to make a list of pros and cons, then that action should be assigned to everyone.

Our action plan should now look something like this:

Action Plan										
Focus: Improve Hazard Reporting and Tracking				**Owner:** Lisa Buck						**Date Created:** 1/1/2021
Team Members: Lisa Buck, Aldrick Lam, Nick Marquart, Jordan Schoyen, and Connor Gagnon										
Background: The facility currently utilizes paper forms that employees use to report hazards. Those paper forms are then routed to the maintenance department for corrective action. However, it is difficult to track the status of corrective actions and parts that have been ordered. Employees are not able to check the status themselves.										
Objectives: Determine what is needed to improve the current process for reporting and tracking hazards to completion. Procure new software (if needed), train employees, and implement new process.			**Timeline**							**Status**
			Proposed Completion Date	Shaded--original plan, X = Complete						Red (incomplete) Yellow (in progress) Green (complete)
				2021						
Action Steps	**Owner**	**Deliverable**		**Jan**	**Feb**	**Mar**	**Apr**	**May**	**Jun**	
Pro and Con List	Lisa Buck	Develop a list of Pros and Cons of current system	1/31/2021							
Pro and Con List	Aldrick Lam	Develop a list of Pros and Cons of current system	1/31/2021							
Pro and Con List	Nick Marquart	Develop a list of Pros and Cons of current system	1/31/2021							
Pro and Con List	Jordan Schoyen	Develop a list of Pros and Cons of current system	1/31/2021							
Pro and Con List	Connor Gagnon	Develop a list of Pros and Cons of current system	1/31/2021							

Status

Now that we know who will be involved and what our first action is, we can add another action to our plan, such as previewing software designed specifically for this purpose. This step will also give us ideas regarding other, newfound inconsistencies within hazard reporting.

Again, if I am expected to set up the demonstration, but everyone else is expected to attend, then your action plan should be updated to reflect those items.

Here is what our action plan looks like now:

Action Plan										
Focus: Improve Hazard Reporting and Tracking			**Owner:** Lisa Buck							**Date Created:** 1/1/2021
Team Members: Lisa Buck, Aldrick Lam, Nick Marquart, Jordan Schoyen, and Connor Gagnon										
Background: The facility currently utilizes paper forms that employees use to report hazards. Those paper forms are then routed to the maintenance department for corrective action. However, it is difficult to track the status of corrective actions and parts that have been ordered. Employees are not able to check the status themselves.										
Objectives: Determine what is needed to improve the current process for reporting and tracking hazards to completion. Procure new software (if needed), train employees, and implement new process.			**Timeline**							**Status**
			Proposed Completion Date	Shaded--original plan, X = Complete						Red (incomplete) Yellow (in progress) Green (complete)
				2021						
Action Steps	**Owner**	**Deliverable**		**Jan**	**Feb**	**Mar**	**Apr**	**May**	**Jun**	
Pro and Con List	Lisa Buck	Develop a list of Pros and Cons of current system	1/31/2021							
Pro and Con List	Aldrick Lam	Develop a list of Pros and Cons of current system	1/31/2021							
Pro and Con List	Nick Marquart	Develop a list of Pros and Cons of current system	1/31/2021							
Pro and Con List	Jordan Schoyen	Develop a list of Pros and Cons of current system	1/31/2021							
Pro and Con List	Connor Gagnon	Develop a list of Pros and Cons of current system	1/31/2021							
Demo of software	Lisa Buck	Set up demo, invite team	2/15/2021							
Demo of software	Nick Marquart	Attend demo	2/15/2021							
Demo of software	Jordan Schoyen	Attend demo	2/15/2021							
Demo of software	Connor Gagnon	Attend demo	2/15/2021							

Status

Now, you've heard me say that documentation is important (many times), but **documenting your action plan is a great way to see how far you've come.** It can also show whether or not the action plan has worked.

If one of your actions for a risk-reduction process is to have workers wear gloves at all times to prevent hand injuries, but once implemented, it did not change the number of injuries—then you know your action plan didn't work. This is yet another reason why we don't want to take on too many actions at one time. If we make a change, we need to measure whether it's successful or not, which can take weeks or months. If you already moved on to the next action, you could have to do it over again. Frustrating!

Now, you're probably thinking that it's a lot of work to put these action plans together, but really, **they only take a few minutes once you have the template.** You also don't need to create an action plan for everything you do. I don't typically document action plans for small tasks that I complete myself, such as updating policies or implementing a small process change. I usually focus on plans that will involve multiple actions or people. I jot down those actions and who is expected to complete each item.

These types of action plans are also great for working on a project with multiple departments. If I have a project on forklifts, propane, or lockout/tagout, I usually enlist team members from other departments to help execute the work.

At one facility I worked at, we had to make various changes to the electrical safety program. The changes were significant and would take up to several months to implement. I met with the maintenance manager to discuss developing an action plan to help us stay on track.

One benefit of this action plan was its accessibility; we uploaded it to SharePoint or Microsoft Teams so that both of us could provide updates. We met every two weeks, to discuss the status of current action items, who was working on them, and if we were on track.

Once, we had a major delay receiving equipment from a vendor and had to extend our deadline for implementation. This then delayed the next action item which was to train workers how to use the equipment. You can see how important it is to stay on track and complete actions in order. If we had already scheduled training, we would have had to cancel or reschedule it; this could be costly if an outside vendor or contractor is scheduled to conduct the training.

Luckily, we had originally decided to not schedule training until all equipment was received and onsite. We saved time and money by simply doing a little planning.

Summary

You may still not be convinced to put action plans together for some of your projects.

- I suggest you start small by creating an action plan for a current project. Document the team members and actions you are already taking. You'll see how easy it is!
- Imagine that OSHA shows up at your facility to conduct a programmed inspection, and they discover some violations. Let's assume you have a documented action plan to address the issues related to their findings. If you didn't have the documented action plan, you may not be able to prove all the work you've been doing. To avoid costly fines, it is super critical to be able to prove your actions.

Action Plan Template

Action Plan											
Focus:			Owner:								Date Created:
Team Members:											
Background:											
Objectives:			Timeline								Status
			Proposed Completion Date	Shaded—original plan, X = Complete							Red (incomplete) Yellow (in progress) Green (complete)
				2020							
Action Steps	Owner	Deliverable		Jul	Aug	Sept	Oct	Nov	Dec		

Status

It is extremely important to get the proper training and to follow instructions—no matter how insignificant they may seem.

CAN YOU HEAR ME NOW?

Early in my Navy career, I learned a valuable lesson about communication. I was a new plane captain on the flight line. My role was to stand in front of the airplane and give hand signals to the pilot to prepare for flight. My squadron was a training squadron for pilots who wanted to learn how to fly this particular aircraft. These hand signals were critical; they determined when to start the engines and when to drop the tail hook (used when planes land on an aircraft carrier). Each hand signal, in my mind, was a well-crafted symphony in a specific order; however, certain pilots didn't always feel the same. They were cocky and thought of themselves as above us—the enlisted plane captains who were simply there as a nicety.

One night in early September, one of my least favorite pilots came out for a launch. Prior to flight, the pilot and I walked the plane to check for any damage or safety concerns. Everything looked good, so the pilot went into the plane to begin the preflight process. At night, pilots cannot see your hands, so plane captains must use lighted wands (the ones that look like a cone on a flashlight). The signals are slightly different at night; the pilot uses a similar light to give signals back to the plane captain.

Unfortunately, this pilot refused to use his light and instead used only his hands to give me signals; I couldn't see any of them. It was extremely frustrating. If I didn't properly understand the signals, it would be my coworkers outside the plane who would be in danger; they perform troubleshooting during start-up.

I felt that the pilot didn't care about anyone's safety, only about getting the plane off the ground. I just stood there as he gave me unintelligible hand signals. I decided that if/when he chose to give the **proper** hand signals, only then would I respond. I could tell he was agitated, with his jerking hand movements, but I didn't budge. As a side note, there is a large hangar that sits alongside the flight line that has an upper level where other pilots are briefed on their particular mission. These pilots can watch other planes launch as they are getting ready.

I was getting aggravated; since I could not decipher his hand signals, I created a few of my own. I used my wands to give the pilot a series of signals; he suddenly stopped to contemplate what I was motioning, but gave no further response. I simply repeated the hand signals.

One of the troubleshooters outside of the aircraft started laughing. The troubleshooter had a radio in his headset. The pilot had apparently communicated the problem to other pilots in a nearby hangar, which overlooked the flight line. Eventually, the obstinate pilot began using proper hand signals. I was able to finish the launch sequence and taxi the plane down the runway for take-off.

As I walked off the flight line, the troubleshooter told me what happened. The pilot wasn't able to understand any of my hand signals. To try to figure out what action to take, he had then called over to the pilots in the hangar; he wanted to see if they understood. When I repeated the signals, one of the pilots said, "I believe she wants you to do the YMCA." That's when he finally got the hint that I refused to act on the improper hand signals.

Needless to say, I was in a little trouble after this incident. I had a meeting with the squadron safety officer to explain how seriously we took hand signals; he offered a solution. He called a safety stand-down with all the pilots (nearly 300—yikes!). I had to stand in front of them in this huge auditorium and review the hand signals for the launch sequence. It was mortifying! Thankfully, after that review, none of my fellow plane captains had any problems with pilots using improper signals, especially at night!

So...what did I learn from this experience? First, **it is extremely important to get the proper training and to follow instructions—no matter how insignificant they may seem.** There are steps to follow in every process; each is as important as the last. These processes protect workers in many fields—not just general industry or construction. **It is so important that we practice, provide feedback, and follow-through.**

Looking back, I should have stopped the launch and sent someone into the plane to speak with the pilot. There were barriers at the time, which caused me to lack confidence; many of the pilots made plane captains feel petty or insignificant, which created a somewhat difficult work environment. This type of environment can exist anywhere, even in your workplace!

When I must deal with a similar situation now, I handle it very differently. I stop the work, and ask questions; I know that I'm doing the right thing for my fellow employees. It is really important to immediately set ground rules in any situation, to ensure everyone is on the same page.

As an example, when I started a new position with a company, there was some high-risk work to be done. I called a brief meeting to review the plan. Well, actually, there was no plan. I talked to the team involved, and we wrote out a short plan to include a timeline and the order of work to be performed. I set the expectation that should anyone have any questions or concerns, we would not keep it to ourselves. We would call a meeting, even if only for a few minutes, and to discuss the issues.

I explained that so many incidents occur because someone saw something out of place and yet didn't say anything. That's why the Department of Homeland Security started the "If You See Something, Say Something" campaign. It really does work!

In this particular case, one of the team members had a question about the delivery and operation of a large crane to be brought on-site. After reviewing the timeline, we realized there would be traffic around the same time, due to the delivery of raw materials. This would cause congestion around the crane while in use, putting the project and workers at risk.

We immediately met with the logistics manager, and rescheduled a few loads for the following day. If the worker hadn't said anything, we may have still gotten the work done, but at what expense?

Our team set the ground rules upfront; we recognized the worker, and the rest of the team, for being proactive. **Each small success must be celebrated.** Make it a big deal by bringing in donuts or another reward the following day; it's a small gesture that makes a huge impact.

Another way to recognize the team is at the beginning of the shift the next day. Bring up the issue, how it was addressed, and why it was important to change the plan. For this example, we reviewed a recent crane incident in our city where major damage and injuries occurred. Make an impact by **thanking employees for speaking up** and shaking their hand. If someone exhibits other-than-positive behavior, you should address that behavior in private. We never want to embarrass a worker or cause them stress by publicly correcting their behavior. **When one person succeeds, the team succeeds, too!**

You may be thinking that you don't have tons of time on your hands to communicate face-to-face at every meeting or discussion, or that you may not be on-site when a safety issue occurs. There are so many great ways to communicate now with **email, texting, instant messaging, video chatting, etc.** If a safety issue arises while someone is out in the field, have them video chat you using FaceTime, Microsoft Teams, Skype, etc.

A few months back, one of our facilities in another state had an issue requiring my attention. The team sent me some photos of the issue, but it was really hard to determine the risk and corrective action from the pictures alone. I asked the team to video chat me from the field, so that I could truly see what was going on. Not only did it help me identify potential risks, but I was able to discuss corrective actions with the team while they were on location.

The employees who brought up the risk were present and involved in the discussion, which helped us to get their buy-in for implementing change. Rather than 15 emails back and forth, we were able to come up with a plan in just one video call. The feedback from the team was overwhelmingly positive; now, they ask if they can video chat me whenever a question arises—which I love!

Many safety professionals have a newsletter to communicate their recent activities, accomplishments, or outstanding action items; this can be a great communication platform. But do workers read it? How do you measure whether employees read your newsletter?

My advice is to always implement activities that positively impact your workers, but you must measure their success! **Each time you publish your newsletter, have a contest or prize associated with the material.** For example, at the end of the newsletter, have a short form for them to fill out, using the newsletter as a guide. Ask a few questions that can be answered by simply reading the newsletter. Have employees turn it in for a chance to win a prize.

Remember—you need to **provide the incentive** for them to learn or read the information. Have you ever received one of those Nielsen television surveys in the mail? They always include a $1 bill. This gives you an incentive to fill it out. If you fill it out and return it to them, they send you $5 more! Obviously, Nielsen has done their research to know that people are motivated by money and are more likely to fill out a survey if incentivized by it.

Think of your newsletter the same way. Do you want employees to read it? Does it include valuable information? If the answer is YES, then incentivize them! And then…yes, you guessed it, **keep the form they turn in as participation documentation.** You're getting the hang of it now!

Another big, communication mistake I see safety professionals make is the posting of safety results, updates, and activities on a pretty bulletin board, which they expect employees to read. Why is it important for employees to read it? What is in it for them?

The safety professional does all this work to update the bulletin board with information sadly just for the employee to ignore. Once again—incentivize them to know the info. A couple of ways to do this is through a survey or contest. Put some forms in high-traffic areas such as the lunchroom or near the time clock. Create the form as a "fill-in-the-blank," where employees fill in the blanks using information posted on the bulletin board. Establish a deadline for workers to turn in their forms, followed by a drawing for tokens or other small prizes.

This is a win-win situation for you. The employee comprehends the information and also gets a chance to win a prize for participating. It's a great way to promote involvement and get employees to review pertinent information.

Summary

- Communication is something we can always improve upon. Now, more than ever, there are more ways to do so. Don't assume that workers have read your email, newsletter, or bulletin board. Go out to their work area, and ask them if they read it. If they didn't...you know you have work to do.

We often
throw so many
corrective
actions at the
problem but,
they aren't the
right actions.

IF IT DOESN'T WORK, QUIT DOING IT

Have you ever had to do something you thought was a waste of time? Me, too! At one of my jobs, I had to prepare a letter each week summarizing my activities. As a department leader, we sent these weekly recaps to a team consisting of about 60 people. This weekly letter took a few hours to prepare; I had to run reports, review the week's activities, and spend time adding descriptive commentary. I felt these letters were an absolute waste of time. All of the managers spent hours every Friday preparing this letter and sending it.

Honestly, I never read any of the other managers' letters. I was at the facility all week; I already knew what happened. I also knew where to get the data that was in the weekly letter. For example, I had a summary of the safety work orders that had been entered and completed. This information was available daily in several meetings and through the work order system that everyone used. Rather than teaching employees where to access the information, it was "easier" to keep summarizing it all for them. Every. Single. Week.

I brought up this issue of time wasted in a leadership meeting with my peers. I told the group that I could do some mini training sessions and develop one-point lesson plans to explain how and where to get the data. My boss was not on board. As it turns out, he reads them every week to ensure we're on track. I thought to myself, **"If he does read them, I think he is the only one."** I decided an experiment was in order to prove that no one read this weekly letter.

The following week, I added these words to the safety work order summary: "If you are reading this, please see me for a FREE candy bar."

You may be wondering, of the 60 employees that received this weekly letter, just how many actually came to me for the free candy bar? Four. Four people, and not one of them was my boss.

So, again, the next week, I added a picture with the caption: "If you are reading this, please see me for FREE cookies."

Can you guess how many came this time? Seven, including the original four. Again, not one of them was my boss. I ran the same 'free treats' program for a month and never had more than 10 people respond. And you guessed it—not one them was my boss.

I brought this subject up yet again at another leadership meeting, which was held four weeks after I started my weekly letter challenge. At first, I only restated that I didn't think anyone was reading the weekly letters. My boss reminded me of our last conversation, claiming that he read them. I had printed out all four of the last weekly letters and highlighted the part where I asked employees to seek me out for 'free treats.' I explained that only about 10% of the staff responded, including my peers. My point was not to embarrass anyone, but to convey that my time could be better spent impacting a higher percentage of people.

Fortunately, I had a great boss and team. We had a laugh before deciding to eliminate the weekly letters and find an alternative way to communicate. I was thankful we were able to change policy and stop wasting time on something that didn't drive results.

Now, not all bosses will be this receptive (thank you, Mark!). Your boss could be royally ticked off that you brought up the subject a second time. You may want to approach your team or boss in private to discuss your findings. Remember to explain why change is needed. In this case, I explained that it took all of the managers several hours to put this information together each week, and our time was better spent working on more meaningful tasks. **I gave my boss examples of what I could be doing instead of writing the weekly letter**, such as assisting employees, developing training, and providing recognition for a job well done. Overall, I was happy with the results of my speaking up; plus, the other managers thought I was pretty cool for helping them out!

At another company facility, I was tasked with coaching a person on my safety team named Joe. He was struggling with a string of recent injuries and needed some guidance. I sat with Joe, and we went over what he was currently working on. He told me there was an issue with employees failing to report injuries. Joe took action by hanging up a dozen signs that said, "If you are injured at work, notify your supervisor immediately."

I asked him if he spoke to the employees about the signs. He said, "Why would I? The signs are there for them to read."

I explained that there are so many signs, labels, and warnings, etc. plastered all over the facility. It begins to look like wallpaper and blend together, rendering them unnoticeable. To get employees to read the signs, simply ask them if they have seen the new signs you hung up. Communicate the purpose of the signs, the expectations, and what to do if they have questions.

I told him that another way to get employees to be more aware is to have a small contest. If new signs are hung in the facility, ask employees where they're located, and reward workers for finding them. By actively looking for the signs, they will become more aware of the sign's message.

Be consistent. Every time new signs are hung; challenges are posted; or changes are communicated; I speak with employees. I make sure they know I care about them and want them to learn all safety program updates in the facility.

Joe had an injury at his facility where a worker stepped on a nail; it went through the shoe, resulting in a recordable injury (one that requires medical treatment). He was shocked that such an injury could have occurred. I was equally shocked, but not by the injury.

All the behavioral safety data Joe received indicated that nails were on the floor. Joe had even purchased magnetic brooms to help stop the nails from accumulating on the floor (from wooden box repairs). Joe said that to address the issue, he would improve magnetic sweeping time—instead of every hour, sweeping would be every 30 minutes.

I asked Joe how many nails on average accumulate in an hour. He couldn't tell me. I asked how many nails accumulated in 30 minutes. He didn't know that either. I explained that he shouldn't make a change until he has acquired more data.

First, if we discover there's an average of 40 nails on the floor per hour, this data would allow us to start an action plan. It is so critical to acquire accurate measurements; this eliminates the need for a do-over!

Second, the nails should be counted during the proposed time of 30 minutes. If there is still an average of 20 nails on the floor, are we truly reducing the hazard to a reasonable level? If the increase of cleaning or sweeping nails doesn't address the issue, then maybe personal protective equipment, such as puncture resistant insoles, are needed for workers in that area.

One of the biggest issues I have seen is that our safety professionals are desperate to solve problems quickly. **They often throw so many corrective actions at the problem but, they aren't the right actions.** Joe told me he was doing more "stuff" than he has ever done. I had to explain to him that it was the wrong "stuff," and that it was not addressing the problems or root cause of the injuries or issues.

We oftentimes make this error by thinking that the more we do, the better off we are. This is not always the case. Take a good hard look at what you are doing. Does it seem like you have a lot of actions (**update SOPs, hang signs, do more training, etc.**)? At times, these are great, but you need to carefully measure the actions you take.

Another employee, DeAnne, was busy creating this elaborate bulletin board near the timeclock in her facility. DeAnne posted safety statistics, the number of days since their last lost time injury, and injury summary reports. She wanted all the employees to see the posted information; however, employees would simply pass by her beautifully curated bulletin board each shift without a second thought.

When we talked about the bulletin board, she was frustrated. She asked, "Why aren't the employees reading my bulletin board? I put so much time and effort into it."

I told her that most employees want to know what's in it for them. What will they gain by reading it? What is the incentive to take a few minutes out of their day to read it understand the information?

I always go back to my reward challenges. If DeAnne posts new information each month, she should create a fill-in-the-blank form. To complete the challenge, employees must use information found only on the bulletin board. This gives each worker an incentive to seek out the information. I have found that filling in the blanks forces workers to read the sentence, not just copy down answers. Raffle off a few prizes, tokens, or snacks at the end of the month; this way, employees will know that there's something in it for them.

Another way to incentivize workers is to have managers hit the floor and ask employees about the bulletin board information. Managers can ask specific questions about the data; if employees respond with the correct answer, they get a token, raffle ticket, etc. If they get the answer wrong, then the manager can tell the employee to seek them out once they have learned the correct answer. After reporting back, they then, of course, get their reward. This process engages the entire staff and keeps employees "in the know" regarding safety.

Summary

- We have so much to do as safety professionals, and continuing to do things that don't move the needle to compliance or injury reduction is silly. Evaluate what you are doing—especially those tasks that take a significant amount of time each day, week, or month. Talk to your teams; determine what activities are more value-added and continue to do them. It won't be easy to change policies or practices that have been in place for years, but if you want to improve, push hard to eliminate waste!

We must
set our
supervisors
up for
success!

FRONTLINE SUPERVISORS GET A BAD RAP

One of the most critical roles in safety is that of the frontline supervisor. As you can tell from the title of this chapter, they tend to get a bad reputation for **not** holding workers accountable, enforcing safety rules, or encouraging participation in the safety program. First, let's take a look at what could cause this behavior, in order to provide suggestions for improvement.

Hourly workers often transition into frontline supervisor roles; they are suddenly thrust into leadership, without any adequate training. It's difficult to go from being "one of the team" to being the leader—now responsible to hold "the team" accountable. There may be a few formal training classes that newly promoted supervisors can take on leadership or time management, but generally there aren't any on leading among an hourly workforce. As I have mentioned, workplace safety is hard, and it sucks! If workers are not interested in the safety program, it only makes it harder on supervisors.

In other cases, supervisors may have been hired from another company or have recently graduated college. This, too, can cause problems, as they may not understand the expectations of the company or the safety challenges they will face with the workforce. **We must set our supervisors up for success!**

I can think of a time when the company I worked for had an issue with a supervisor; the supervisor was improperly submitting incident reports. The plant manager kept complaining that reports were not submitted on time; but, when I checked with the supervisor, he still didn't have access to the online system to submit them! How can we set expectations when we have not provided all the necessary tools?

We should always provide the proper training and tools for employees to do their job. How can we expect someone to do their job per the Standard Operating Procedure (SOP), or complete a Job Hazard Analysis (JHA) if they don't even have the forms or access to the proper paperwork?

This is no different for supervisors—we must ensure they have the correct tools to perform their work.

What about hands-on training? Should we partner a newly hired supervisor with an experienced one, to show them the ropes? Shouldn't we take the time to show them the correct actions to take?

In the earlier example, does the new hire have a supervisor's guide, which shows the proper incident report process including deadlines for submission? We can do a better job by creating a plan for each supervisor.

If you don't already have a training plan for your supervisors to conduct safety-related tasks, the following topics can act as your starting point. You will also want to add topics such as coaching employees on safety risks; leading safety/leading by example; and follow-through for risk identification and corrective action.

First, create a binder with different sections for each safety topic. Below is my go-to list for supervisor training:

- **Incident investigations.** Supervisors should understand the expectations of their role when it comes to investigating incidents. This goes for all types: property damage, near misses, first aid, recordables, contractor incidents, temporary worker incidents, etc. In some cases, supervisors may be asked to take pictures and provide details to a temporary employee agency or contractor. With full-time employees, they may be expected to complete a full report and investigation.

  What about root cause analysis (RCA) exercises? I can't tell you how many times we have asked a supervisor to perform a root cause analysis, and they have no idea how to do it! Make sure to go over these procedures and practice—it's a time commitment upfront, but the reward is worth it.
- **Emergency response.** Training should include the supervisor's role in each potential emergency. If he or she is responsible to take a headcount and call emergency services, then this should be documented in the training. Also, if the supervisor is expected to know the fire pump or fire panel location, then walk around the facility and physically show him or her the equipment.

  Scenarios are the best way to describe what the supervisor should do and how to handle a situation. If the supervisor is expected to write a summary report after the incident or turn in paperwork for additional follow-up, make sure to include this in the training. The new hire may also be expected to learn CPR, first aid, and how to operate an AED in an urgent situation.

- **Confined Spaces.** Many times, frontline supervisors are used as entry supervisors for permit-required confined space entries. This is a critical role and topics should include their role and responsibilities for performing the duties of an entry supervisor. Remember that supervisors must ensure employees terminate the permit when required, or work is completed, and turn in their paperwork. I prefer that workers turn in their completed confined space permits to the supervisor for review prior to submission to the safety office. It gives the supervisors an opportunity to review the permit with their team and correct any errors or omissions before I receive it.
- **Permit Programs.** Supervisors must know their specific responsibilities for all types of work, including each type of permit (red tag, line break, hot work, etc.) they may authorize. They may need to witness or participate in certain activities to gain knowledge and experience. For example, if a supervisor is expected to authorize a line break permit, is he or she aware of the potential hazards present? Does the supervisor have the knowledge or experience to identify issues? Additional training with maintenance and/or engineering may be necessary to understand the process and to discover potential hazards.
- **General program oversight.** This topic includes understanding proper procedures for lockout/tagout, electrical safety, PPE, etc. Supervisors need in-depth training on safety policies in order to ensure employees follow the rules. A good way to educate supervisors is to have them take an online training class with a related quiz (or create a short quiz after you present the policy

information). You can then review where weaknesses exist, or if there is an area requiring further explanation.

- **Behavioral safety.** Many companies now use some form of behavioral safety observation. These peer-to-peer observations are typically conducted in work areas while employees perform their normal tasks. The role of the supervisor is to ensure employees have ample time to complete their observations, review the data, and coach observers on how to improve the observation process.
- **Coaching and discipline.** The role of the supervisor may be to coach or discipline employees who have committed a safety infraction. The training binder should include a copy of the disciplinary protocol or employee handbook that outlines appropriate steps to take. It is also important that supervisors understand how to properly collect data and facts in order to make an educated decision.

  A good way to practice coaching or disciplining workers is to role play. It can be very difficult to confront an employee who has violated a safety rule, or put himself or others in danger. Employees can sometimes attempt to deflect or, blame others, or simply not take responsibility for their actions. It takes practice to ensure that the supervisor is fair and consistent and learns how to control the coaching or discipline meeting. Learning how to turn a negative into a positive during these types of interactions is critical to the success of the safety program. Getting employees to commit to taking the proper safety precautions in the future should also be a focus of these types of meetings. Another critical talking point for supervisors is how to stop at-risk behaviors while they are happening. We should teach supervisors how to promptly react and stop dangerous behaviors without freaking out, yelling, or scaring workers. Again, role playing can be super helpful to show supervisors exactly how you expect them to react.

As an example, if a supervisor sees a worker not wearing appropriate PPE when required, how should he or she react to the situation? Should the supervisor yell at them? Stop the work? Scold the worker on the spot? Or, should the supervisor calmly ask the worker to stop their work and step away to discuss in private **(this one!)**? Teaching supervisors exactly the behavior you want is critical.

- **Leadership training.** When should a safety stand-down be conducted? What should the messaging be to the crew? Supervisors should be trained to handle serious situations and communicate appropriately with their team. Give supervisors examples of when to conduct a safety stand-down and how to be honest with their team, without giving too many details regarding the situation.
- **Engaging and rewarding workers.** Be clear on your expectations for engaging workers in the safety program. Do you want supervisors to help their team with the monthly safety challenges? Or support employees during a changeover? Guiding employees can be tricky, and we need supervisors to keep workers focused on identifying and correcting hazards.

  Do you want supervisors to share incident reports from other sites with their teams? How should they present and document that the information was shared? You must train them how to do so.

Plus, don't forget to convey the expectations around rewards and recognition. It isn't easy for everyone to provide praise. Give supervisors examples of desired, positive behaviors, and include them in the binder.

Summary

- **Be kind to your supervisors!** They work hard managing everything from staffing to payroll to getting product out the door. They help employees, and we need their leadership—especially when it comes to workplace safety.

In my opinion, both SHARP and VPP are excellent programs to pursue.

IS WORLD-CLASS SAFETY A THING?

I'm so excited that you made it this far! I previously mentioned that I had the opportunity to lead two manufacturing plants (two different companies) to achieve the **Safety and Health Achievement Recognition Program (SHARP)** as well as the **Voluntary Protection Program (VPP) Star** certifications. If you aren't familiar with these, they are cooperative programs with OSHA for companies that demonstrate exemplary workplace safety programs. There are different levels to the VPP, including Merit, Demonstration, and Star. Nevada only has the VPP Star, which is the highest level of achievement. There are so many amazing benefits to these programs, such as a decrease in injury rates and exemption from OSHA's programmed inspections. In this chapter, I will share my thoughts and experiences in the process of achieving these coveted certifications. I also encourage you to research the requirements for your area, as they can vary by state.

The first time I was interested in working toward achieving the VPP Star certification was with a pulp and paper company in Nevada. We had a very good safety culture with a low incident rate. We had other sites within our company that had already achieved the VPP certification, so I had an idea of what it took to maintain such a certification. You might have noticed I used the word "maintain." That is because I really had no idea how to begin the process! At the time, there weren't many manufacturing VPP sites in Nevada for me to reach out to for guidance. It ended up taking much longer than I anticipated to build a foundation for the program and to figure out what worked and what didn't.

In my opinion, both SHARP and VPP are excellent programs to pursue. They will push you to establish a partnership with your hourly team or enhance the one you already have. When I first conducted an internal audit of a VPP Star site in Idaho, I was amazed. Processes in place there were missing at my location. Employees were super engaged, and management was really involved in the identification and correction of hazards. I interviewed many workers during that audit, and they highly praised the safety program—I wanted a culture like that! I was jealous of what they had and wanted it for myself and my facility.

I eventually partnered with my counterpart in Idaho, Cindy, my very first mentor, who gave me advice and lots of support (I needed it!). I also had complete support from our entire company to pursue the VPP certification, so there were no hurdles from that perspective.

I initiated the process by reaching out to the Nevada VPP program coordinator. At the time, the state of Nevada was going through some very difficult challenges, so the coordinator didn't provide much direction; however, the coordinator did provide me with the application format, and told me to reach out to another VPP site for help.

As it turns out, this was good advice. I was able to contact two other locations and visited both sites for a tour and review of their documentation. They had incredible programs, which again, really fueled my desire to push forward. I learned a few valuable lessons early on, one being to document everything! I talked about the importance of documentation in the chapter "You Can't Tell OSHA Your Dog Ate It."

It took a very long time to earn my first VPP certification—six years, actually. That's way too long for a site that already had an excellent safety record. The first few years were spent learning the requirements of the VPP from other sites and colleagues. They had specific practices in place that we didn't have, such as confined space rescue teams, lockout/tagout audits, and excellent hourly employee engagement.

Figuring out what would work at our facility and within our operating budget was challenging. Building trust and participation was critical to our success. I doubted myself plenty of times and kept thinking, "We aren't ready." My advice to you is that nothing will ever be perfect, but it does needs to be great. Improving the process of attaining VPP Star happened while pursuing the certification the second time.

Shortly after achieving VPP Star, I had the opportunity to take on a new role with a beverage facility, again in Nevada. This location suffered a fatality in the previous year, which I was aware of when accepting the position at that plant. A few of my coworkers asked me if I was making the right decision leaving a VPP Star site to start a new job at a plant that recently had a fatality. I thought that if anyone could turn that plant around, it would be ME! During my interview, my new boss had specifically asked about my VPP experience, and if it was something I was interested in working toward again. Of course, my answer was yes!

I applied lessons from my first attempt at VPP, which included beginning with the SHARP certification. What's great about SHARP is that the Safety Consultation and Training Section (SCATS) helped us identify our program gaps. **The service is completely free, and they do not communicate with the enforcement side of OSHA (unless you completely fail to address hazards).**

Each state is a bit different and may have a completely separate entity that handles consultations. Companies can invite SCATS to come in and review a single program, such as lockout/tagout, or have them conduct a full, comprehensive inspection. I have to say that although I had full support from my boss to invite OSHA into the plant to conduct an inspection, the corporate team was initially not aligned. They were hesitant to open our plant to scrutiny, but after a little negotiation, we got their approval.

I opted to have SCATS complete the comprehensive inspection with the knowledge that we wanted to pursue SHARP. In my experience, the consultation team reviewed our policies and procedures, and conducted an inspection of our facility. This process took approximately one year and was very helpful. They conducted sampling, interviewed employees, and inspected every inch of our facility. At each visit, they identified hazards we needed to correct. This is a formal process where the company must respond with corrective action within a specified time frame.

The SCATS team used Form 33 (linked at LisaKnowsSafety.com) which is a **gap analysis form**. This analysis helped us establish a baseline; the same form was used again to evaluate our facility at the end of the process. There are specific criteria that must be met (including injury rate) to achieve the SHARP certification.

The entire facility team knew that once we achieved SHARP, we would continue to move toward the VPP Star certification. Employees were already used to change, new systems and procedures, and they understood the need to keep progressing.

The criteria for achieving VPP Star are more stringent and tougher to achieve than the SHARP certification. You've heard me say it over and over in this book, but I'll say it again: you must document everything! If you say you have done something—you must be able to prove it.

In my opinion, there is one major difference between the two programs; **for VPP, you should establish double protection for your programs, policies, tasks, and compliance.** As an example, if you have a calendar with reminders about when training is due, you should have a redundant system. I use a compliance calendar, my personal calendar, **and** our training software. This way, if I am no longer with the company, important information will not be lost with my separation; it leaves a slim chance for required training to fall through the cracks.

Achieving the VPP Star certification took another two years, which was a huge improvement from the initial six. Since I had already implemented many best practices during my first VPP certification, I knew what needed to be done. **We completely flipped from having a fatality to becoming a VPP Star site.** Employees were so proud—their hard work had paid off!

When I started with the company and conducted new-hire orientation, workers would ask me about the fatality, mentioning they read something online. One newly hired worker asked me,

"Is this a safe place to work? I have a family. I can't afford to work where it isn't safe." I assured the worker that we had a plan to address and eliminate hazards.

After achieving the VPP Star certification, new hires would instead ask me about the VPP flag or mention the latest news article on our safety successes. Our achievements didn't just affect our employees, but the views of others on our company and culture.

Summary

- Yes—world-class safety exists!
- You know by now that I am a huge advocate of employee involvement! I've provided so many great ideas in this book to get you started. Finding multiple ways to involve employees, lead safety, and educate are critical to the success of cooperative programs. Determine what works for your facility and how to get employees engaged. Tweak some of the ideas I've given you to best fit your needs and most importantly—have fun on your safety journey!

CONCLUSION

This book is unique in its approach to safety. It's the culmination of my 20+ years of experience, hard work, frustrations, and lessons learned—all documented to help you engage your employees, improve safety results, and develop your own enviable safety culture.

At times, we as safety professionals or leaders must search for ideas to get employees interested in safety; it can be hard, invasive, and most importantly, no fun. I don't want you to go through some of the struggles I encountered early in my career—that's why I wrote this book.

This is the book I wish I'd had when I first started. Despite your best efforts, you'll inevitably meet someone who does not share your enthusiasm for safety. Whenever you find that challenging or unmotivated person, consider your reaction. Don't let people like this get you down or make you want to give up your job. Leading safety is tough and doesn't have to be part of your job title. You just have to want to protect people. And you never know—one of those people just might be you.

Made in the USA
Columbia, SC
13 July 2024

38570341R00093